THIS BOOK BELONGS TO:

NAME:

_____

GRADE:

_____

TEACHER:

_____

SCHOOL:

_____

G.L.A.T. Science

Practice Test Workbook

Grade 6

Authored by Bahamian Teachers United

Published by BSM Consulting

Copyright © 2020/2021

All Rights Reserved.

ISBN: 978-1530555901

DISCLAIMER: This book has been adapted from the G.L.A.T. Science Papers for Grade 6. The questions have each been modified slightly in adherence to the copyright laws of The Commonwealth of The Bahamas.

TABLE OF CONTENTS

1. Circle the response below that best represents the basic unit of a leaf, a mushroom and a dog.

   (A) Spore

   (B) Colony

   (C) Pseudopod

   (D) Cell

2. Which of the following organisms have cells that are surrounded by a cell wall?

   (A) Beetle   (B) Horse   (C) Fern

3. Which of the lists below represents the most basic to the most complex structures found in organisms?

   (A) Cells: Tissues: Organs

   (B) Organs: Tissues: Systems

   (C) Cells: Systems: Organs

   (D) Tissues: Cells: Systems

4. Which of the following can be found in toothpaste, dishwashing liquid and paint?

(A) Yeast
(B) Bacteria
(C) Diatoms
(D) Amoebas

5. Which of the following statements about viruses is true?
(A) Viruses cause Lyme disease in humans
(B) Viruses must reproduce inside living cells
(C) Viruses are larger than bacteria
(D) Viruses move by forming 'false feet'

6. The fungi kingdom contains which pair of organisms?

(A) Amoeba and Mildew
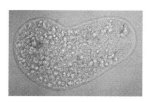 

(B) Yeast and Mold
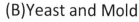

(C) Paramecium and Virus
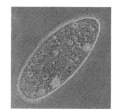 

(D) Mushroom and Diatom

7. Which of the organisms below is made up of a single cell? Circle the correct response.

(A) Amoeba

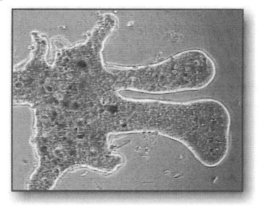

(B) Earthworm

(C) Mushroom

(D) Pine Tree

8. Which of the following characteristics is shared by both planarians and sea stars?

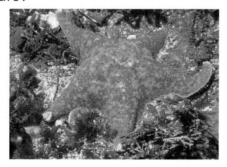

Sea Star

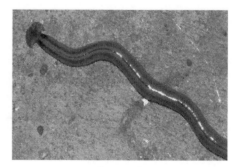

Planarian

(A) Living in streams

(B) Re-growing missing parts

(C) Having shells

(D) Having spiny skin

9. How are sponges and echinoderms alike?

Sponge

Echinoderm

(A) They live in salt water

(B) They are microscopic

(C) They live attached to hard surfaces

(D) They move with tube feet

10. How do the tube feet found on the sea star help it to feed?

(A) They force open clam shells

(B) They suck on animals' blood

(C) They digest food

(D) They pump food and water throughout the body

11. Circle the answer that best represents the characteristics of vines' growth patterns.

    (A) Many short trunks

    (B) Climbing stems

    (C) Long, deep roots

    (D) Needle-like leaves

12. What does soil provide for plants? Circle the correct answer.

    (A) Sunlight

    (B) Oxygen

    (C) Nutrients

    (D) Carbon dioxide

13. What is the process being shown in the picture?

    (A) Gravitropism

    (B) Extinction

    (C) Phototropism

    (D) Geotropism

14. Which of the following is the best definition of 'weather'?

    (A) Atmospheric conditions

    (B) Temperature

    (C) Precipitation

    (D) Land conditions

15. Which of the following instruments measures wind speed?

(A) Hydrometer

(B) Anemometer

(C) Wind Vane

(D) Barometer

16. What do we call scientists who study weather patterns?
    (A) Astronauts
    (B) Biologists
    (C) Doctors
    (D) Meteorologists

17. Which agent of erosion causes the removal of sand from the shoreline?
    (A) Snow
    (B) Wind
    (C) Heat
    (D) Waves

18. What is the name of the process which causes rocks on the earth's surface to change in shape and size?
    (A) Deposition
    (B) Erosion
    (C) Weathering
    (D) Sedimentation

19. Which process describes the transfer of eroded rock?
    (A) Deposition
    (B) Erosion
    (C) Sedimentation
    (D) Weathering

20. Which type of weathering causes damages to buildings and statues?
    (A) Limestone
    (B) Carbon dioxide
    (C) Sand
    (D) Acid rain

21. The solar system consists of many smaller bodies, including planets. What is the name of the body that orbits the sun?
    (A) Coma
    (B) Galaxy
    (C) Earth
    (D) Asteroid

22. Which of the following bodies is made up of rock, ice and frozen gas?
    (A) Meteoroid
    (B) Atom
    (C) Star
    (D) Comet

23. Which of the following bodies has a long tail of gases that glows when it is near the sun?
    (A) Meteor
    (B) Moon
    (C) Planet
    (D) Comet

24. Honey Bunches of Oats is Tyler's favorite breakfast cereal. It consists of nuts, flakes and clusters of oats. What is produced when these ingredients are combined?
    (A) Element
    (B) Mixture
    (C) Molecule
    (D) Solution

25. Iron filings and saw dust were stored in the same container. What is the best method for separating the iron filings from the saw dust?
    (A) Heat the mixture
    (B) Pour water on the mixture
    (C) Use a magnet
    (D) Use a magnifying glass

26. Solutions consist of two main parts, what are they?
    (A) Mixture and solvent
    (B) Solute and mixture
    (C) Solution and mixture
    (D) Solute and solvent

27. When air particles press down on the Earth what is the formed?
    (A) Humidity
    (B) Wind
    (C) Air pressure
    (D) Air temperature

28. During the summer the weather office reports that a warm front is headed toward your island. Which weather could your island experience?
   (A) Cool air
   (B) Blizzard
   (C) Hurricane
   (D) Clear skies

29. Which of the layers listed is closest to the Earth's surface?
   (A) Mesosphere
   (B) Troposphere
   (C) Exosphere
   (D) Stratosphere

30. Which statement best describes the conservation of energy?
   (A) Energy has no beginning or end
   (B) Energy can be created and destroyed
   (C) Energy cannot be created nor destroyed
   (D) Energy is very powerful

31. In the image below, what process is taking place?

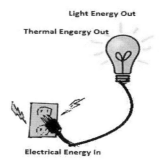

   (A) Electrical energy is changed to light and mechanical energy
   (B) Electrical energy is changed to heat and light energy
   (C) Heat energy is changed to electrical and light energy
   (D) Electrical energy is changed to chemical and mechanical energy

32.Which of the statements below states one use of solar energy in the home?
- (A) To repair appliances
- (B) To build cabinets
- (C) To heat water
- (D) To clean surfaces

33.What occurs when vapor is changed into liquid?
- (A) Precipitation
- (B) Salinity
- (C) Condensation
- (D) Evaporation

34.Which action will result in a product that has new chemical properties?
- (A) Cutting wood
- (B) Breaking a mirror
- (C) Popping popcorn
- (D) Tearing paper

35.A scientist observes the following molecular pattern. What state of matter is being demonstrated?

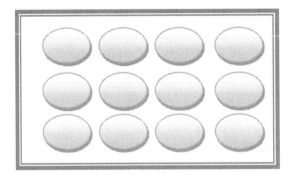

- (A) Vapor
- (B) Solid
- (C) Liquid
- (D) Gas

36. Which of the below elements combine to make molecules?

(A) Atoms

(B) Protons

(C) Neutrons

(D) Electrons

37. What type of substance is made up of one type of atom?

(A) Solution

(B) Mixture

(C) Compounds

(D) Elements

38. Which of the following is a characteristic of metal?

(A) Cannot be polished

(B) Gas

(C) Luster

(D) Brittle

39. Which natural resource does acid rain destroy?

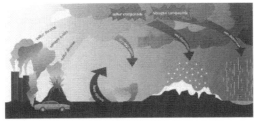

(A) Oil

(B) Plants

(C) Coal

(D) Minerals

40. Fish in a pond are dying. Students realize there is a factory nearby. Which action may be the cause of the fishes' deaths?

(A) Someone threw garbage in the pond

(B) The factory dumps pollutants in the pond

(C) Fishermen are catching all the fish

(D) Plastic bottles are being thrown into the pond

For Answer Key Go To:

http://greatminds.teachable.com/courses/glat-workbook-answer-keys/

May 2011 – Short Answers Questions

WORMS

The diagram shows the characteristics of round worms and segmented worms.

ROUNDWORMS	SEGMENTED WORMS
Have simple body systems	Have complex body systems
Have round, tube-like bodies	Bodies are segmented
Are invertebrates	Are invertebrates
Can be parasites	Can be parasites

1. (a) Name **ONE** similarity between roundworms and segmented worms.

   _____[1]

   (b) Name ONE difference between roundworms and segmented worms.

   _____[1]

2. Write the name of the group to which each of the following worms belongs.

   (a) Leech_____[1]

   (b) Tapeworm_____[1]

3. What is a parasite?

   _____[1]

4. A roundworm was found in the intestine of a cow. Identify which organism is the:

   (a) Parasite_____[1]

   (b) Host_____[1]

5. Identify **ONE** way that human beings can avoid being infected by worms.

_____
_____[1]

6. During a presentation in class, Paula makes a statement that '**all worms are harmful to man and his environment'.** Do you agree with this statement? Give **ONE** reason to support your answer.

_____
_____
_____
_____
_____
_____[2]

Total Marks [10]

For Answer Key Go To:

http://greatminds.teachable.com/courses/glat-workbook-answer-keys/

FROM FLOWER TO FRUIT

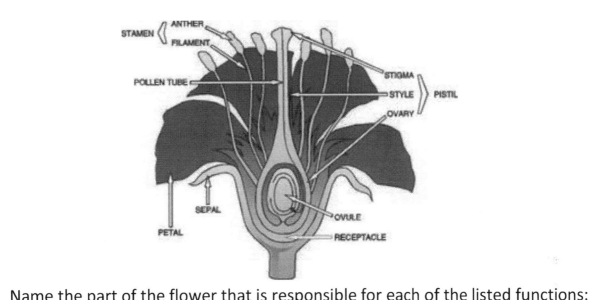

1. Name the part of the flower that is responsible for each of the listed functions:

   (a) Pollen production_____[1]

   (b) Fruit and seed production_____[1]

2. State the function of the following parts of the flower.

   (a) Sepal_____[1]

   (b) Petal_____[1]

3. Which part of the flower do pollen grains stick to?

   _____

   _____[1]

4. What is the scientific name for flowering plants?

   _____

   _____[1]

5. The first important step in seed formation is pollination. What is **'pollination'**?

_____

_____

_____[2]

6. How do bees help in the pollination process?

_____

_____

_____[2]

Total Marks [10]

STORMS

The picture below shows people outside during storm conditions.

1. List TWO weather conditions the people in the picture are experiencing.

    (a) _____[1]

    (b) _____[1]

2. Why is it harmful to be outside during a thunderstorm? Explain in detail.

    _____

    _____

    _____

    _____

    _____[2]

3. Name ONE way the weather conditions shown are affecting the umbrella the lady in the picture is holding.

    _____

    _____[1]

4. Name **TWO** conditions that are necessary for a storm to develop into a thunderstorm.

_____

_____

_____

_____[2]

5. Name TWO types of storms other than thunderstorms that people in the Bahamas can experience.

(a)_____[1]

(b)_____[1]

6. What instrument is used to measure rainfall?

_____[1]

Total Marks [10]

For Answer Key Go To:

http://greatminds.teachable.com/courses/glat-workbook-answer-keys/

MOTION AND FORCES

1. Define the term 'force'.

   _____

   _____

   _____

   _____[2]

2. List two things that force can cause an object to do.

   _____

   _____

   _____

   _____[2]

3. You sit on a chair. Your weight is force acting on the chair. What force is acting on you?

   _____

   _____[2]

The diagram shows THREE different types of forces

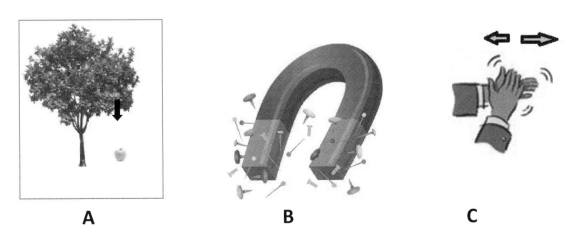

A   B   C

4. Name the type of force shown in the above 3 diagrams (A, B and C)

    A _____   [1]

    B _____   [1]

    C _____   [1]

5. State the type of force that does each of the following:

(a) Hold objects to the Earth's surface_____[1]

(b) Acts directly on objects which are in contact_____[1]

Total Marks [10]

For Answer Key Go To:

http://greatminds.teachable.com/courses/glat-workbook-answer-keys/

1. (a) Name the form of energy shown in the diagram.

   _____[1]

   (b) How is this form of energy produced?

   _____[1]

2. Based on the students' positions labeled 'A', 'B' and 'C' in the picture:

   (a) Which student hears the softest ringing of the bell?

   _____[1]

   (b) Which student hears the loudest ringing of the bell?

   _____[1]

   (c) Explain why it is possible for the action in 1 (a) and 1 (b) to happen.

   _____

   _____[2]

3. Explain why a flash of lightening is seen before a clap of thunder is heard.

_____

_____[1]

4. Write one word from the box to match each of the statements in the table.

Sound	Pitch	Echo	Wave

A. Causes a series of vibrations	
B. How high or low a sound is	
C. A reflection of sound waves	

[3]

Total Marks [10]

For Answer Key Go To:

http://greatminds.teachable.com/courses/glat-workbook-answer-keys/

PLANTS AND HUMAN LIFE
The pictures below show three different plants

Aloe **Cotton** **Corn**

1. Name the plant that provides the materials to:-

   (a) Make medicine_____[1]

   (b) Feed humans and livestock_____[1]

   (c) Make clothing_____[1]

2. Name TWO products other than clothing that can be made from a tree.
   (a) _____[1]

   (b) _____[1]

3. What is the main use of plant products in The Bahamas?
   _____[1]

4. What is the name given to scientists who study plants?
   _____[1]

5. Grapes are purchased in different forms, colors and sizes. Name one way that scientists have changed the varieties of grapes grown.
   _____[1]

6. Scientists have developed a product from the corn plant that is capable of soaking up more than 300 times its own weight in water. Explain how the use of this product can:

(a) Help babies

_____[1]

(b) Help the environment

_____[1]

Total Marks [10]

1. Which of the following is the basic structural unit of all organisms?
   (A) Blood
   (B) Cells
   (C) Heart
   (D) Vein

2. Which plant structure controls the cell's activities?
   (A) Nucleus
   (B) Chloroplast
   (C) Cytoplasm
   (D) Vacuole

3. What type of fungi is a parasite?
   (A) Mushroom
   (B) Mildew
   (C) Yeast
   (D) Mold

4. Which of the following creatures is a vector invertebrate?
   (A) Butterfly
   (B) fly
   (C) cricket
   (D) spider

5. Which of the following diseases is spread by the Aedes Egypti mosquito?
   (A) Malaria
   (B) Yellow fever
   (C) Dengue fever
   (D) Rabies

6. Which cells destroys bacteria and germs in the body?
   (A) Skin cells
   (B) White blood cells
   (C) Red blood cells
   (D) Nerve cells

7. Which type of chemical do white blood cells produce in the body?
   (A) Saliva
   (B) Tobacco
   (C) Iron oxide
   (D) Antibodies

8. What is the primary function of the body's immune system?
   (A) Causes illness in the body
   (B) Contributes to thinking in the body
   (C) Protects the body from illnesses
   (D) Produces energy for the body

9. The body receives support and protection from which of the following body systems?
   (A) Respiratory system
   (B) Circulatory system
   (C) Skeletal system
   (D) Digestive system

10. The lungs are protected by which of the following bone structures?
    (A) Wrist bone
    (B) Rib cage
    (C) Spinal column
    (D) Cranium

11. Which mineral is the most abundant mineral found in human beings?
    (A) Potassium
    (B) Calcium
    (C) Sodium
    (D) Magnesium

12. Nicholas planted seeds in a Styrofoam cup. After a period of time the seeds started to sprout. What is the name given to this process?
    (A) Germination
    (B) Evaporation
    (C) Fermentation
    (D) Precipitation

13. Nicholas observed the sprouting seeds for changes? Which of the following parts of the plant did Nicholas see growing first?
    (A) Roots
    (B) Flowers
    (C) Stems
    (D) Leaves

14. Which of items listed gives a seed the energy it needs for growth and development?
    (A) Mineral salts
    (B) Starches
    (C) Sunlight
    (D) Soil

15. Which of the following processes shows the flow of energy through the food chain?
    (A) Sun: herbivores: carnivores: producers
    (B) Sun: carnivores: producers: herbivores
    (C) Sun: producers: carnivores: herbivores
    (D) Sun: producers: herbivores: carnivores

16. Which animal best completes the flow of energy in the food chain below?

SUN ⟶ CABBAGE ⟶ ? ⟶ BIRD ⟶ PEOPLE

    (A) Caterpillar
    (B) Alligator
    (C) Snake
    (D) Bear

17. Which picture below shows a wetland ecosystem?
    (A) Desert
    (B) Deciduous forest
    (C) Flower garden
    (D) Flamingo pond

18. Most weather changes occur in which layer of the atmosphere?
    (A) Thermosphere
    (B) Mesosphere
    (C) Stratosphere
    (D) Troposphere

19. Weather stations utilize a number of instruments? One of them is shown in the diagram below. What does it measure?

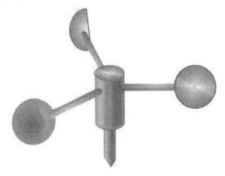

    (A) Wind direction
    (B) Air pressure
    (C) Rainfall
    (D) Wind speed

20. How does the atmosphere offer benefit to the earth?
    (A) It protects the earth from other planets
    (B) It protects the earth from cold weather
    (C) It protects the earth from water
    (D) It protects the earth from harmful sun rays

21. Which of the natural disasters below is the least dangerous?
    (A) Tornado
    (B) Hurricane
    (C) Tsunami
    (D) Thunderstorm

22. Which of the following reduces the strength of hurricanes?
    (A) Rain and sun
    (B) Rivers and ponds
    (C) Land and cold water
    (D) Land and hot water

23. Which safety precaution should you take if you get caught outside during a thunderstorm?
    (A) Wait out the storm under a tree
    (B) Play on the playground
    (C) Lie flat on the ground
    (D) Wait out the storm near a lamp pole

24. You are observing stars from your back yard? Why do some of them appear to shine brighter than others?
    (A) They are larger
    (B) They are smaller
    (C) They are further away from the earth
    (D) They are closer to the earth

25. Brianne's dad studies stars. What is his professional job title?
    (A) Astronaut
    (B) Botanist
    (C) Astronomer
    (D) Geologist

26. Andre's class is observing the moon through a telescope. How does the use of this instrument help him?
    (A) It makes the moon look fuller
    (B) It makes the moon look closer
    (C) It makes the moon look bigger
    (D) It makes the moon look brighter

27. Which of the following can be found both on Mars and on Earth?
    (A) Rain
    (B) Oil
    (C) Oceans
    (D) Volcanoes

28. The following table shows some facts about Earth and Venus? Which of the facts shows the greatest difference?

Planet	Mass	Diameter	Density	Surface Temperature
Earth	1.100	12,756	5.50	56°C
Venus	0.82	12,104	5.24	470°C

    (A) Mass
    (B) Diameter
    (C) Density
    (D) Surface Temperature

29. Clouds bring rain and snow on the Earth? How do these elements contribute to life on earth?
    (A) They cool the land
    (B) They build up on mountains
    (C) They give fresh water to organisms
    (D) They carry acid to soil

30. Which of the following resources is not easily replaced?
    (A) Renewable energy
    (B) Non-renewable energy
    (C) Nuclear energy
    (D) Natural energy

31. Why are coal and oil not easily replaced once used?
    (A) They take millions of years to form
    (B) They form under high pressure
    (C) They are burned up to produce energy
    (D) They are buried deep in the earth

32. If you breathe on a mirror, water droplets form? What is this an example of?
    (A) Evaporation
    (B) Boiling
    (C) Freezing
    (D) Condensation

33. Sharon puts a thermometer in a glass filled with hot water. Why does the liquid in the thermometer rise?
    (A) Air pressure above the water pulls it up
    (B) Gravity pushes it up
    (C) Air bubbles are released
    (D) Heat from the water causes it to expand

34. If a crayon is melted which **TWO** properties remain the same?
    (A) Mass and color
    (B) Temperature and hardness
    (C) Shape and physical state
    (D) Thickness and texture

35. When paper is folded which physical property is changed?
    (A) Shape
    (B) Texture
    (C) Magnetism
    (D) Color

36. Which of the following shows a chemical change?
    (A) Torn paper
    (B) Air escaping from a balloon
    (C) Ice melting
    (D) Scratched match

37. Which of the following apparatus is used to measure volume?
    (A) Ruler
    (B) Balance scale
    (C) Spring scale
    (D) Graduated cylinder

38. Which characteristic is used to describe the motion of an object?
    (A) Shape
    (B) Speed
    (C) Color
    (D) Length

39. Which substance is normally used to reduce friction?

(A) Oil

(B) Salt

(C) Air

(D) Dust

40. Which floor surface would make it rather difficult to pushing a piano?

(A) Smooth cement

(B) Thick rug

(C) Bare wood

(D) Flat tiles

For Answer Key Go To:

http://greatminds.teachable.com/courses/glat-workbook-answer-keys/

May 2012 – Short Answer Questions

SPONGES

The diagram below shows sea sponges.

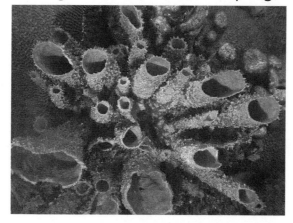

1. What are the tiny holes or openings called that cover the sponges' surface?

   _____[1]

2. A sponge has numerous structures. Name the structure that has the function of removing water from the sponge.

   _____[1]

3. What is the name of the habitat where most sponges are found?

   _____[1]

4. Sponges are filter feeders. Describe the process of 'filter-feeding'.

   _____[1]

5. Why are sponges classified as animals?

   _____

   _____

   _____[2]

6. Identify **ONE** way in which natural sponges can be used.

   _____

   _____[1]

7. All sponges reproduce. What type of reproduction provides the greatest freedom for sponges? Give reasons why.

_____

_____

_____

_____

_____

_____[2]

Total Marks [10]

For Answer Key Go To:

THE CIRCULATORY SYSTEM

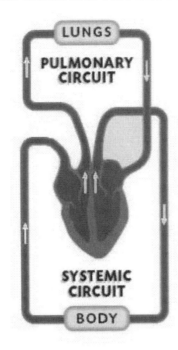

1. Describe the main function of the circulatory system.

   _____[1]

2. Name the main organ of the circulatory system.

   _____[1]

3. Name the largest artery found in the circulatory system.

   _____[1]

4. What is the blood cell responsible for the following functions?

   (a) Carrying oxygen and carbon dioxide   _____[1]

   (b) Fighting diseases   _____[1]

5. List TWO unhealthy habits that can cause harm to the circulatory system.

   (a) _____[1]
   (b) _____[1]

6. Name one form of heart disease.

_____[1]

7. List TWO differences between a vein and an artery.

_____

_____[2]

Total Marks [10]

For Answer Key Go To:

http://greatminds.teachable.com/courses/glat-workbook-answer-keys/

BIOMES

The picture below shows a biome.

7. This biome has 3 forest layers. What is the name of this biome?

_____[1]

8. Name another biome that has forest layers.

_____[1]

9. Circle two animals below that lives in the biome pictured.

CAMEL	MONKEY
TOUCAN	SHEEP

10. Andre conducted biome research for a science project. He discovered the biome in the picture has more plants and animals in it than another other biome. Explain why this is the case.

_____
_____
_____[2]

11. Organisms living in different types of biomes have to adapt to their environment for survival. Complete the below chart which shows the biomes and their adaptations of the organisms.

Name of Biome	Organism	Adaptation
________________	Polar Bear	________________
________________	Cacti	________________

Total Marks [10]

For Answer Key Go To:

http://greatminds.teachable.com/courses/glat-workbook-answer-keys/

POLLUTION

The diagrams show THREE types of pollution.

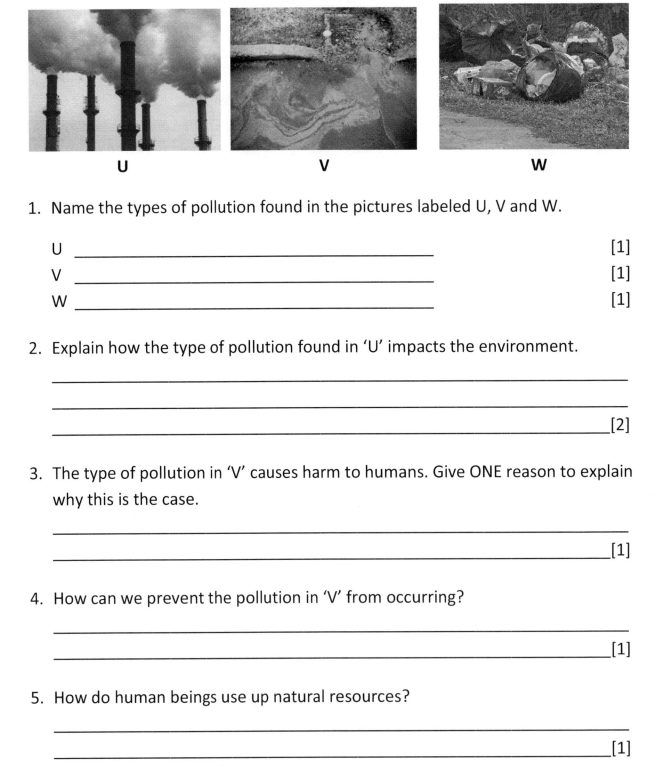

| U | V | W |

1. Name the types of pollution found in the pictures labeled U, V and W.

   U _____ [1]

   V _____ [1]

   W _____ [1]

2. Explain how the type of pollution found in 'U' impacts the environment.

   _____

   _____

   _____[2]

3. The type of pollution in 'V' causes harm to humans. Give ONE reason to explain why this is the case.

   _____

   _____[1]

4. How can we prevent the pollution in 'V' from occurring?

   _____

   _____[1]

5. How do human beings use up natural resources?

   _____

   _____[1]

6. Scientists have identified ways to conserve natural resources; these are known as the 3R's. Name one of the 3R's and explain what it means.

_____

_____

_____[2]

TOTAL MARKS [10]

For Answer Key Go To:

http://greatminds.teachable.com/courses/glat-workbook-answer-keys/

MAGNETISM

The diagram shows a magnet and its lines of force

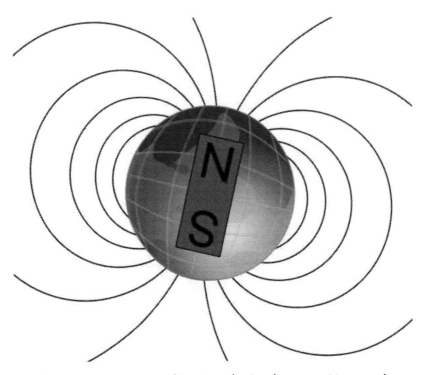

1. Magnets are given names according to their shapes. Name the magnet in the picture.

   _____[1]

2. Name another type of magnet.

   _____[1]

3. Name the planet that is a huge magnet.

   _____[1]

4. Name the magnetic force of this planet?

   _____[1]

Use the words below to answer question 5.

coins	pins	erasers	marbles

5. Name TWO objects that can be attracted by magnets.

   (i) _____ [1]

   (ii) _____ [1]

6. What do you call the area around a magnet?
   _____[1]

7. Where is this area felt the strongest on a magnet?
   _____[1]

8. If two magnets are placed together with the north ends of both facing each other, describe what happens.
   _____[1]

Total Marks [10]

For Answer Key Go To:

http://greatminds.teachable.com/courses/glat-workbook-answer-keys/

ELECTRICAL CIRCUITS
The diagram below shows a simple circuit

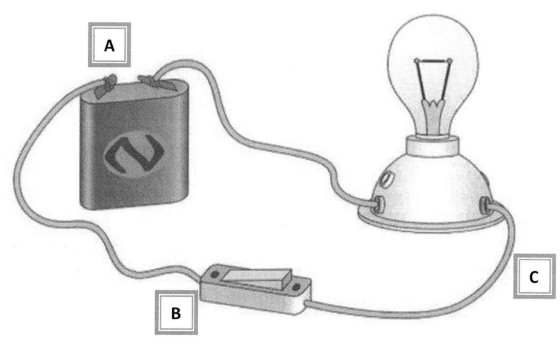

5. Name the parts of the circuit labeled 'A', 'B' and 'C'.

    A   _____   [1]

    B   _____   [1]

    C   _____   [1]

6. Write the letter of the path that best matches each statement.
   (i)   Provides the power source _____[1]
   (ii)   Path for electrons to flow _____[1]
   (iii)   Opens or closes the circuit _____[1]

7. When the switch is closed what happens to the light bulb?

   _____[1]

8. Name the object that does not allow electrons to flow through it easily.

   _____[1]

9. From the list below, write down the name of the object that is the best conductor of electricity.

Plastic	glass	copper

_____[1]

10. Mr. Saunders works at an electrical plant. He wears rubber gloves every day at work. Why do you think Mr. Saunders wears these gloves on a daily basis?

_____

_____[1]

Total Marks [10]

For Answer Key Go To:

http://greatminds.teachable.com/courses/glat-workbook-answer-keys/

1. The first person to describe cells was Robert Hooke. Which instrument did he make his observations with?
   (A) Spring scale
   (B) Telescope
   (C) Magnifying glass
   (D) Microscope

2. Michael is looking at animal cells. He is observing the structure responsible for controlling what enters and leaves the cell. Which structure is he looking at?
   (A) Nucleus
   (B) Cell membrane
   (C) Vacuole
   (D) Cell walls

3. Which of the following invertebrates is most likely found in a marine environment?
   (A) Earthworms
   (B) Ants
   (C) Sea anemone
   (D) Spiders

4. Which of the following invertebrates is classified as a crustacean?
   (A) Lobster
   (B) Centipede
   (C) Butterfly
   (D) Ant

5. Which of the following muscles lines the intestine and also moves food through the digestive system?
   (A) Involuntary
   (B) Smooth
   (C) Skeletal
   (D) Cardiac

6. Which muscle in the body causes the movement of limbs and other parts of the body?
   (A) Involuntary
   (B) Smooth
   (C) Skeletal
   (D) Cardiac

7. A sugar apple fruit represents which part of the flower?
   (A) Seed
   (B) Bud
   (C) Stamen
   (D) Anther

8. In what type of environment would you find animals that are adapted to prevent water loss?
   (A) Grassland
   (B) Desert
   (C) Tropical Rain Forest
   (D) Deciduous Forest

9. Which of the following plants is indigenous to the Bahamas?
   (A) Hibiscus
   (B) Casuarina
   (C) Pigeon Plum
   (D) Brazilian pepper

10. In the Bahamas, what type of medicinal plant is used to treat the common cold?
    (A) Sage
    (B) Life Leaf
    (C) Cerasee
    (D) Fever Grass

11. Why is photosynthesis important for plants?
    (A) It rids the plant of waste
    (B) It attracts insects to the plant's flowers
    (C) It helps the plants produce its foods by trapping sunlight
    (D) It produces chemicals from plant sugar

12. Which gas in used up during the process of photosynthesis?
    (A) Hydrogen
    (B) Carbon dioxide
    (C) Oxygen
    (D) Carbon monoxide

13. What is the name given to the small openings in leaves that take in carbon dioxide?
    (A) Stomata
    (B) Xylem
    (C) Phloem
    (D) Chloroplast

14. Which of the following biomes has a climate similar to the one in The Bahamas?
    (A) Desert
    (B) Deciduous Forest
    (C) Tropical Rain Forest
    (D) Grassland

15. Brianne and her friends measure the daily temperature at school for Science class. Which weather instrument do they most likely use?
    (A) Hydrometer
    (B) Anemometer
    (C) Barometer
    (D) Thermometer

16. Which instrument is used to collect data from the following picture?

(A) Barometer
(B) Wind vane
(C) Anemometer
(D) Rain Gauge

17. People from colder climates are sometimes not used to the high humidity in the Bahamas. What does the term **'high humidity'** mean?
(A) A cool temperature
(B) A high pressure system
(C) An approaching cold front
(D) A large amount of water vapor in the air

18. What type of professional informs the community about the weather forecast in a given area?
(A) Meteorologist
(B) Astronaut
(C) Paleontologist
(D) Botanist

19. Angela notices a smooth, huge rock with a hole in it. Which of the following processes caused a change in the rock's appearance?
(A) Erosion
(B) Weathering
(C) Sedimentation
(D) Deposition

20. The roof of Robyn's house was damaged by Hurricane Irene. Which of the following erosion agents most likely caused the damage?
(A) Water
(B) Wind
(C) Ice
(D) Heat

21. Which mineral can be found in abundance in the ocean?
(A) Oil
(B) Silver
(C) Calcium
(D) Gold

22. Which of the following fuels is the main source of transportation energy?
(A) Coal
(B) Petroleum
(C) Biomass
(D) Natural gas

23. Which of the following fossil fuels is used in the production of steel?
(A) Gas
(B) Oil
(C) Diesel
(D) Coal

24. Which of the following objects can be found in the Solar System between the Mars and Jupiter belt?
(A) Comets
(B) Planets
(C) Meteors
(D) Asteroids

25. Which of the following is used as a navigational tool?
    (A) A comet
    (B) A star
    (C) An asteroid
    (D) A meteoroid

26. When Tenaj's brother followed her directions to the playground, he was in motion? 'Motion' is described as any change of:
    (A) Speed
    (B) Acceleration
    (C) Position
    (D) Force

27. What type of ball requires more force to move than a soccer ball?
    (A) Hockey ball
    (B) Bowling ball
    (C) Tennis ball
    (D) Golf ball

28. Which of the words below means 'the power to work'?
    (A) Mass
    (B) Distance
    (C) Friction
    (D) Energy

29. Which type of energy is displayed by a car at the highest point of roller coaster ramp?

(A) Magnetic energy

(B) Chemical energy

(C) Kinetic energy

(D) Potential energy

30. Which of the following will create the most amount of friction by pushing a piece of furniture across it?

(A) Carpet

(B) Vinyl

(C) Ice

(D) Wood

31. A doorknob is part of which simple machine?

(A) Wheel & axle

(B) Lever

(C) Pulley

(D) Load

32. Which machine listed below is best used for raising and lowering light objects?

(A) Engine

(B) Fixed pulley

(C) Wheel & axle

(D) Movable pulley

33. Which example of a simple machine allows you to put force on one side so that you can do work or move a load on the other?

(A) Wheel & axle

(B) Pulley

(C) Lever

(D) Motor

34. The instrument in the diagram measures matter. Which of the following properties of matter does it measure?

(A) Mass
(B) Texture
(C) Shape
(D) Size

35. Antoine adds a teaspoon of salt to a cup of water. What is the water an example of?
(A) A solute
(B) A solvent
(C) A liquid
(D) A mixture

36. A student listed to an mp3 player. Which type of energy is represented by the playing mp3 player?
(A) Nuclear
(B) Sound
(C) Radiant
(D) Chemical

37. Dora is building an energy efficient house in The Bahamas. What form of energy would be the best option for her home?
(A) Hydroelectric energy
(B) Solar energy
(C) Electrical energy
(D) Nuclear energy

38. When we drive around the streets of Nassau, gases and bits of dust go into the air. What substance forms as a result of this action?
    (A) Smoke
    (B) Acid rain
    (C) Clouds
    (D) Rain

39. How can people contribute to land pollution?
    (A) Conserving
    (B) Recycling
    (C) Littering
    (D) Reusing products

40. What effect can garbage or solid waste have on the ocean?
    (A) Coral reefs can sink
    (B) Animals can strangle and die
    (C) Plants can be poisoned
    (D) The water can dissolve

For Answer Key Go To:

http://greatminds.teachable.com/courses/glat-workbook-answer-keys/

May 2013 – Short Answer Questions

INVERTEBRATES

The diagram below shows a number of invertebrates.

Sea Cucumber   **Sea Urchin**   **Starfish**

1. What is the name given to the group of invertebrates these animals belong to?
   _____[1]

2. Name another organism that belongs to the group named in question 1.
   _____[1]

3. Give one difference between this group of invertebrates and other invertebrates.
   _____[1]

4. How do sea urchin and starfish protect themselves from predators?
   _____[1]

5. The starfish has the ability to regenerate its body parts.
   (a) What does the term 'regenerate' mean?

   _____
   _____[2]

   (b) State one way the starfish benefits from regeneration.

   _____
   _____[1]

6. Starfish move using their 'tube feet'. Give one other purpose these tube feet serve

_____

_____[1]

7. The group of animals shown has a unique system of canals that help with their movement. Describe how this process works.

_____

_____

_____

_____

_____[2]

Total Marks [10]

THE IMMUNE SYSTEM
The diagram shows parts of the Immune system.

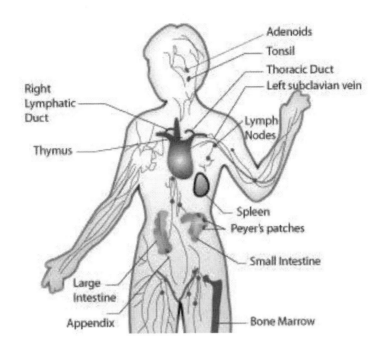

1. What is the main purpose of the Immune system?

_____[2]

2. How do medicines assist the Immune system in carrying out its functions?

_____[1]

3. Name the drug that can cause a decline in brain cell activities when overused in humans.

_____[1]

4. Rashaan has the flu. Describe what occurs with the white blood cells in his body.

_____

_____[2]

5. Viruses are responsible for some of the diseases found in the body. Describe what is happening with the virus in each of the steps below.

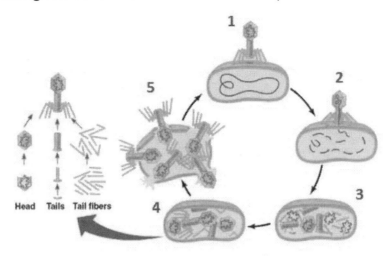

STEP 1 _____

STEP 2 _____

STEP 3 _____

STEP 4 _____

STEP 5 _____

_____[3]

6. Children in the Bahamas are immunized before going to school for the first time. Explain why this process is important.

_____

_____

_____[2]

Total Marks [10]

ATMOSPHERIC LAYERS
The diagram below shows atmospheric layers.

Earth's atmosphere

Exosphere

Air temperature decreases with height

500-600 km.   Termopause

Air temperature increases with height   Termosphere   Ionosphere (radio propagation, Auroras)

International Space Station

80 km.   Mesopause

Air temperature decreases with height   Mesosphere

Km above sea live

50 km.   Stratopause

Air temperature increases with height   Stratosphere   Ozone layer (Absorbing ultraviolet solar radiation)

10-18 km.   Tropopause

Air temperature decreases with height   Troposphere

Sea level

1. What is the atmosphere?
_____[1]

2. Which layer holds the air we work, play and live in?
_____[1]

3. What role do the Ionosphere ions play in making technology usage possible?

_____

_____

_____[2]

4. What is the difference between weather and climate?

_____

_____

_____[2]

5. What are TWO conditions that affect weather?

    (i) _____

    (ii) _____   [2]

6. Ozone is found in the stratosphere. Define the term ozone.

    _____[1]

7. Why is the ozone layer in the stratosphere necessary?

    _____[1]

Total Marks [10]

For Answer Key Go To:

http://greatminds.teachable.com/courses/glat-workbook-answer-keys/

LAYERS OF THE EARTH
The diagram shows the earth's layers.

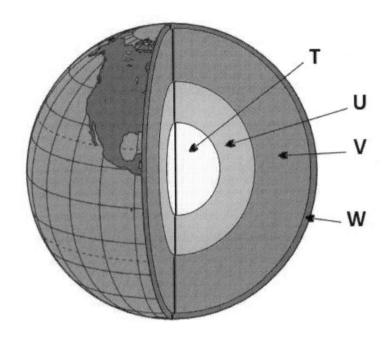

1. Name the layers labeled T, U, V and W.

   T _____ [1]

   U _____ [1]

   V _____ [1]

   W _____ [1]

2. What is magma and where can you find it?

   _____

   _____

   _____[2]

3. Different minerals can be found in the earth's crust. Name one and indicate its use.

   _____

   _____[2]

4. The earth's outer layer is comprised mainly of rocks. These rocks are classified into three main categories. Name them.

(a) _____ [1]

(b) _____ [1]

(c) _____ [1]

TOTAL MARKS [10]

For Answer Key Go To:

http://greatminds.teachable.com/courses/glat-workbook-answer-keys/

MATTER

The diagrams demonstrate physical and chemical changes in matter.

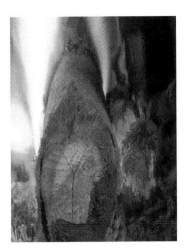

A   **B**

1. Write the letter of the picture that shows
   (a) A physical change in matter _____[1]
   (b) A chemical change in matter _____[1]

2. Examine pictures 'A' and 'B' closely.
   (a) What is the cause of the change in picture 'A'?
   _____[1]

   (b) Explain the change occurring in picture 'B'.
   _____[1]

3. What type of matter is formed from the changes taking place in picture 'A'?
   _____[1]

4. Give the scientific definition of matter.

_____

_____[1]

5. A picture of a bicycle is shown below.

Give TWO physical properties of a bicycle.

(i) _____ [1]

(ii) _____ [1]

6. Describe how the frame of the bicycle can be:

(i) Changed physically

_____[1]

(ii) Changed chemically

_____[1]

Total Marks [10]

ENERGY CONSERVATION

The pictures below show different sources of energy.

1. Name **THREE** energy sources shown in the pictures.
   a) _____ [1]
   b) _____ [1]
   c) _____ [1]

2. Which of the energy sources above is most difficult to replace?
   _____[1]

3. Name two problems fossil fuels can cause.

   _____

   _____

   _____[2]

4. Every day we waste water. Name two ways to conserve water in our homes.

_____

_____

_____[2]

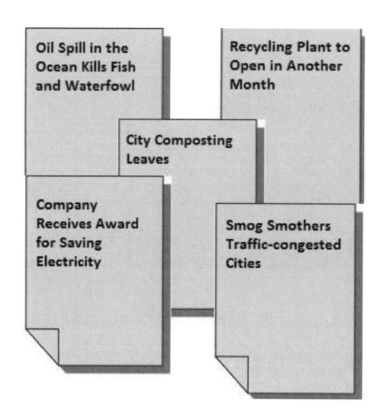

5. Study the newspaper headlines. Give TWO conclusions that can be drawn from these headlines regarding the people in this community.

_____

_____

_____

_____

_____[2]

Total Marks [10]

For Answer Key Go To:

http://greatminds.teachable.com/courses/glat-workbook-answer-keys/

1. Which of the following invertebrates transmits the germ that causes dengue fever?
   (A) Cockroaches
   (B) Flies
   (C) Mosquitoes
   (D) Spider

2. What will the draining of a pond in a mosquito infested are prevent?
   (A) Condensation
   (B) Deposition
   (C) Germination
   (D) Reproduction

3. Which parts named below can only be found in a plant cell?
   (A) Cell membrane and nucleus
   (B) Cell wall and cytoplasm
   (C) Cell wall and chloroplast
   (D) Chlorophyll and vacuole

4. Which of the following parts is responsible for controlling cell reproduction?
   (A) Chlorophyll
   (B) Cytoplasm
   (C) Nucleus
   (D) Vacuole

5. Which of the following structures in the plant cell is responsible for food production?
   (A) cell membrane
   (B) chloroplast
   (C) nucleus
   (D) vacuole

6. Which of the following is **NOT** a function carried out by the skeletal system?

    (A) Allowing for body movement

    (B) Circulating blood throughout the body

    (C) Protecting the body's main organs

    (D) Supporting the body's weight

7. Which of the organs below is the rib cage responsible for protecting?

    (A) Brain

    (B) Kidneys

    (C) Lungs

    (D) Stomach

8. Calcium helps human beings maintain strong, healthy bones. Which of the following foods does not contain a good source of calcium?

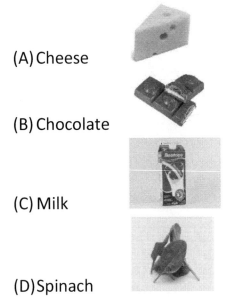

    (A) Cheese

    (B) Chocolate

    (C) Milk

    (D) Spinach

9. Which of the following will NOT negatively impact the ecosystem?

    (A) Adding chemicals to the soil

    (B) Cutting trees down

    (C) Planting a flower garden

    (D) Polluting the water system

9. The following is a list of endangered species. Which of them is a large rodent?
   (A) Flamingo
   (B) Hutia
   (C) Iguana
   (D) Green sea turtle

10. Rock Iguanas do well in dry, sandy patches and limestone rocks. These types of habitats help Rock Iguanas survive because?
    (A) They represent good breeding grounds
    (B) They keep the Rock Iguana moist
    (C) They provide a good source of hydration
    (D) They provide food for the iguana

11. Which of the plants listed is adapted to living in a pond?
    (A) Cactus
    (B) Fern
    (C) Coconut trees
    (D) Water lilies

12. Pine trees are designed with special features that help prevent the loss of water. What are these special features?
    (A) Deep roots
    (B) Needlelike leaves
    (C) Deep roots
    (D) Thick stems

13. Mangroves typically grow in what type of environment?
    (A) Cool
    (B) Dry
    (C) Wet
    (D) Hot

The diagram shows the different parts of the heart.

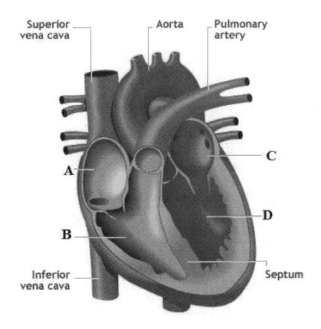

14.(i) Which of the following body systems does the heart belong to?
(A) Circulatory System
(B) Reproductive System
(C) Immune System
(D) Skeletal System

(ii) Give the names of the parts labeled A and C.
(A) Atrium
(B) Chamber
(C) Valve
(D) Ventricle

(iii) Give the names of the parts labeled B and D.
(A) Atrium
(B) Chamber
(C) Valve
(D) Ventricle

15. What is the best way to care for the Circulatory System?
    (A) Take a bath twice a day
    (B) Wash your hands often
    (C) Do regular exercises
    (D) Eat burgers and fried regularly

16. Which type of natural disaster forms an 'eye' once wind speeds exceed 70 miles per hour?
    (A) Earthquake
    (B) Hurricane
    (C) Tornado
    (D) Thunderstorms

17. Which type of natural disaster gives a discharge of electricity?
    (A) Earthquake
    (B) Hurricane
    (C) Tornado
    (D) Thunderstorms

18. What are scientists who study fossils called?
    (A) Astronomers
    (B) Botanists
    (C) Meteorologists
    (D) Paleontologists

19. Sharon found a rock with a dead lizard's imprint on it. Which of the following did she find?
    (A) Cast
    (B) Trace
    (C) Mold
    (D) Excavation

20. On which layer of the earth are continents found?

(A) Inner core

(B) Crust

(C) Mantle

(D) Outer core

21. Which type of natural disasters help scientists collect information about the inner core of the earth?

(A) Tornado

(B) Earthquake

(C) Hurricane

(D) Tsunami

22. The meteorological department reported that the wind was blowing from the southeast. Which weather instrument was used to record this data?

(A) Hydrometer

(B) Anemometer

(C) Wind vane

(D) Barometer

23. What does the instrument in the picture measure?

(A) Wind speed

(B) Air pressure

(C) Humidity

(D) Wind direction

24. What is the name given to the vehicle that is used to explore deep space and planets that humans cannot get to?
(A) Satellite
(B) Space station
(C) Space probe
(D) Space shuttle

25. Which of the instruments below is used to observe distant objects in space?

(A) Binoculars

(B) Microscope

(C) Telescope

(D) Wind vane

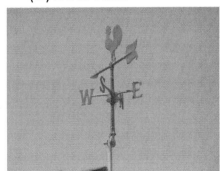

26. The atmosphere consists of a mixture of gases. Which gas makes up the majority of the atmosphere?
(A) Carbon dioxide
(B) Oxygen
(C) Argon
(D) Nitrogen

27. Every day we communicate via telephone and radio. Which layer of the universe makes this possible?
    (A) Exosphere
    (B) Mesosphere
    (C) Ionosphere
    (D) Thermosphere

28. Which of the following provides the energy that moves charges through a circuit?
    (A) Battery
    (B) Switch
    (C) Wire
    (D) Bulb

29. Which of the following materials listed below acts as an insulator?
    (A) Rubber
    (B) Copper
    (C) Wire
    (D) Aluminum

30. When entering or leaving a room, what do you use to turn the light on or off?
    (A) Bulb
    (B) Switch
    (C) Battery
    (D) Wire

31. What is the name of the force that attracts magnets?
    (A) Gravity
    (B) Magnetism
    (C) Friction
    (D) Buoyancy

32. If Anna tries to bring the poles of two magnets together they are repelled by each other or push away. What causes this?
    (A) Unlike poles repel
    (B) Unlike poles attract
    (C) Like poles repel
    (D) Like poles attract

33. Which of the following is an example of a mixture?
    (A) Kool-aid
    (B) Water
    (C) Salt
    (D) Sugar

34. If you wanted to dissolve some salt quickly what type of water would you use?
    (A) Cooled and stirred
    (B) Heated and stirred
    (C) Cooled only
    (D) Heated only

35. Mr. Johnson, a vendor at the fish fry, prepared a delicious tropical conch salad for a customer. What is the tropical conch salad classified as?
    (A) A compound
    (B) A chemical change
    (C) A solution
    (D) A mixture

36. Which of the following is the energy efficient way to dry one's clothing?
    (A) In a clothes hamper
    (B) In a clothes dryer
    (C) With a hot iron
    (D) Outside on a clothesline

37. Which appliance still uses energy even though it is turned off?
    (A) An electric fan
    (B) A microwave
    (C) A toaster
    (D) An electric fan

38. Shonnie likes to conserve energy. Which of the following demonstrates energy conservation?
    (A) Listening to a CD
    (B) Reading a book
    (C) Playing video games
    (D) Watching TV

For Answer Key Go To:

http://greatminds.teachable.com/courses/glat-workbook-answer-keys/

May 2014 – Short Answer Questions

INVERTEBRATES

The diagram below shows a number of invertebrates.

| Crab | Spiny Lobster | Krill |

1. Which group of arthropods do the animals above belong to?
   _____[1]

2. List TWO characteristics of these animals.
   (i) _____[1]
   (ii) _____[1]

3. Name another animal that belongs to this group that is not shown in the picture above.
   _____[1]

4. (a) What is the scientific name for the hard outer covering found on the bodies of the animals in the picture?
   _____[1]

   (b) What the name given to the process where these individuals shed the outer covering?

_____[1]

5. The land crab is most commonly found on which island of the Bahamas?
_____[1]

6. Why is the spiny lobster important to The Bahamian economy?
_____[1]

7. The spiny lobster is protected by law.
   (a) How is the spiny lobster protected by law in The Bahamas?

   _____

   _____[1]

   (b) Why is the spiny lobster protected by law?

   _____

   _____[1]

Total Marks [10]

FUNGI

The diagram shows four types of fungi.

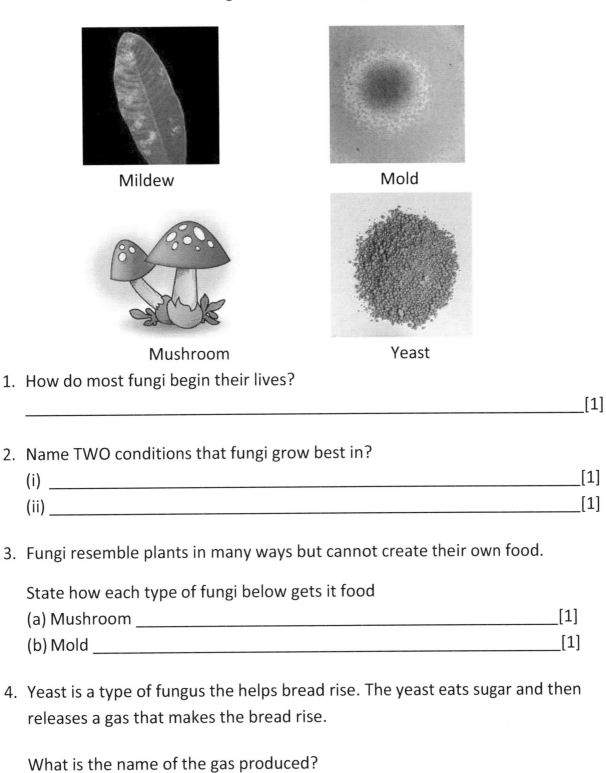

Mildew

Mold

Mushroom

Yeast

1. How do most fungi begin their lives?

_____[1]

2. Name TWO conditions that fungi grow best in?
   (i) _____[1]
   (ii) _____[1]

3. Fungi resemble plants in many ways but cannot create their own food.

   State how each type of fungi below gets it food
   (a) Mushroom _____[1]
   (b) Mold _____[1]

4. Yeast is a type of fungus the helps bread rise. The yeast eats sugar and then releases a gas that makes the bread rise.

   What is the name of the gas produced?

   _____[1]

5. Fungi can become parasites on animals and plants.

   (a) Give an example of a type of fungi that is a parasite.

   _____[1]

   (b) Explain why the fungi you named in (a) is parasitic.

   _____[1]

6. State TWO ways that fungi are beneficial to humans.
   (i) _____[1]
   (ii) _____[1]

Total Marks [10]

For Answer Key Go To:

http://greatminds.teachable.com/courses/glat-workbook-answer-keys/

ATMOSPHERIC LAYERS
The diagram below shows the Solar System

1. Give the names of two inner and two outer planets in the solar system.

	Inner Planets	Outer Planets
Name 1		
Name 2		

[2]

2. What is the main difference between the inner and outer planets in the solar system?

_____

_____

_____[2]

3. What divides the inner and outer planets?

_____[1]

4. Which planet in the solar system has a huge storm system that is comparable in size to planet earth?

_____[1]

5. **'Mars is the planet in the solar system that is most similar to earth.'**
   State TWO ways the two planets are similar to each other?

   i) _____[1]
   ii) _____[1]

6. **'Carbon dioxide has increased in the earth's atmosphere.'**
   Explain TWO ways that the amount of carbon dioxide in the earth's atmosphere can be reduced.

   _____

   _____

   _____[2]

                                                    Total Marks [10]

WEATHERING, EROSION AND DEPOSITION

The diagrams show aspects of weathering, erosion and deposition.

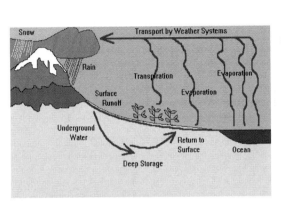

Weathering

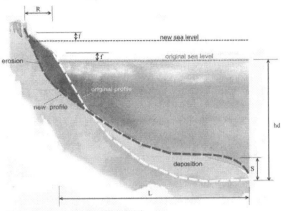

Deposition & Erosion

5. Using the words stated above, write the correct response for each of the following statements.

   a) Movement of broken rocks and soil from one place to another.

   _____[1]

   b) The wearing away or changing of rocks into smaller pieces.

   _____[1]

   c) The carrying of weathered rocks or soil to a new location.

   _____[1]

6. 'Water is an agent of weathering'. List TWO other agents of weathering.
   (i) _____[1]
   (ii) _____[1]

7. As Paula walked along the beach she noticed a large sand hill that was not formed naturally. State one way the hill may have been formed.

   _____
   _____[1]

8. **'Hurricanes have caused lots of damage to coastal areas.'**
   Name a coastal area damage that can be caused by a hurricane

   _____

   _____[1]

9. An earthquake has occurred that is No. 1 on the Richter Scale. Why won't emergency crews be called for assistance?

   _____

   _____[1]

10. 'Water weathers rocks in a number of ways.'

    Explain **TWO** ways in which this process occurs.

    _____

    _____

    _____

    _____[2]

    TOTAL MARKS [10]

For Answer Key Go To:

http://greatminds.teachable.com/courses/glat-workbook-answer-keys/

FRICTION

The diagrams below represent friction occurring on several surfaces.

A. Men on Mountain   B. Car on the bridge   C. Tractor in a field

7. Explain how friction is taking place in each of the pictures above.

Picture A. _____[1]

Picture B. _____[1]

Picture C. _____[1]

8. What does the word **'friction'** mean?

_____
_____
_____
_____[2]

9. Brianne and Nicholas love riding their bicycles.

What happens if they fail to lubricate their bicycles regularly with oil?

_____
_____[1]

10. **'The roads are covered in oil because of a horrible accident.'**

(a) Explain why the roads described above would be difficult for cars to drive on?

_____

_____

_____

_____[2]

(b) Would the roads be easier to drive on if they were covered with grave or sand? Explain your answer.

_____

_____

_____

_____[2]

Total Marks [10]

For Answer Key Go To:

http://greatminds.teachable.com/courses/glat-workbook-answer-keys/

TECHNOLOGY AND FORMS OF ENERGY
The diagram below shows various uses of energy in a home.

1. Name **TWO** forms of energy that is used in the pictures and state their sources.

FORM OF ENERGY	SOURCE OF ENERGY
1.	
2.	

[2]

2. What is the definition of the term **'energy'**?

_____

_____

_____ [2]

3. (a) Name a renewable form of energy that can be added to this home to make it more energy efficient.

_____

_____[1]

(b) Explain how the form of renewal energy in (a) can be used?

_____

_____

_____

_____[2]

4. **'Technology provides the use of energy for many of the things we enjoy in our lives today.'**

State one way technology in energy use has made our lives easier

_____

_____[1]

5. State one way efficient forms of energy can benefit each of the following:
(a) Families

_____

_____[1]

(b) The environment

_____

_____[1]

Total Marks [10]

For Answer Key Go To:

http://greatminds.teachable.com/courses/glat-workbook-answer-keys/

1. **'Tom placed a cell slide under a microscope to determine whether it came from a plant or an animal.'**
   Which of the following cell parts must be present in the cell for it to be a plant cell?
   (A) Vacuole
   (B) Cell Wall
   (C) Nucleus
   (D) Mitochondria

2. What is the jellylike substance in a cell called that is responsible for keeping it functioning?
   (A) Chlorophyll
   (B) Cytoplasm
   (C) Nucleus
   (D) Lysosomes

3. **'Fungi are plant-like organisms that cannot make their own food.'** Fungi are important to ecosystems because they act as:
   (A) Herbivores
   (B) Decomposers
   (C) Producers
   (D) Consumers

4. What type of fungus is used to produce antibiotics?
   (A) Mold
   (B) Yeast
   (C) Mushroom
   (D) Mildew

5. Which organism belongs to the same group as starfish?
   (A) Sea urchin
   (B) Tube sponge
   (C) Conch
   (D) Earthworm

6. Which of the following is **a trait of flatworms**?
   (A) Digestive system with one opening
   (B) Digestive system with two openings
   (C) Segmented body structures
   (D) More complex body systems

7. Which body part is used by this animal for catching food?

   (A) Shells
   (B) Mantle
   (C) Tube feet
   (D) Tentacles

8. Which exercise can be used to strengthen arm muscles?
   (A) Reading a book
   (B) Playing soccer
   (C) Running long distances
   (D) Playing tennis

9. Why is it NOT possible for persons to control their heartbeat?
   (A) The muscles are thick
   (B) The muscles are voluntary
   (C) The muscles are involuntary
   (D) The muscles are weak

10. The organ system that fights off illnesses and diseases in the body is called:

(A) Muscular System

(B) Digestive System

(C) Immune System

(D) Respiratory System

11. **'Nathan's cut became infected because bacteria were trapped in the white blood cells.'**

The yellow-colored material that is formed because of the trapped bacteria is known as:

(A) Plasma

(B) Pus

(C) Platelets

(D) Red blood cells

12. **'Cocaine is an illegal drug found most parts of the world, including the Bahamas'.**

What is another drug that is illegal in The Bahamas?

(A) Cigarettes

(B) Cigars

(C) Marijuana

(D) Alcohol

13. Which of the following terms best describes the **'wise and careful use of plants'**?

(A) Plant germination

(B) Plant pollination

(C) Plant adaptation

(D) Plant conservation

14. Which of the following is **NOT** a plant conservation method?

    (A) Cutting down plenty trees

    (B) Partner with the Bahamas National Trust

    (C) Plant indigenous trees in our yards

    (D) Reduce, reuse, recycle

15. Which of the following plants is considered to be an endangered species in The Bahamas?

A. Hibiscus

B. Lignum Vitae

C. Mango

D. Pineapple

16. Which organism in this food chain is a producer?

Sunlight.........Grass.........Deer...........Coyote..........Earthworm

    (A) Deer

    (B) Coyote

    (C) Grass

    (D) Earthworm

17. **'Spiders prey on insects to survive.'**

    If there is a decline in the insect population what would happen to the spider population?

    (A) It would increase tremendously

    (B) It would decrease tremendously

    (C) It would double

    (D) It would remain the same

18. **'Frogs are eaten by snakes.'**

    Which of the following groups does the frog belong to?

    (A) Decomposers

    (B) Preys

    (C) Predators

    (D) Scavengers

19. Which of the following group of words are representative of the '3 R's of conservation?

    (A) Reduce, Renewable, Recycle

    (B) Reduce, Reuse, Recycle

    (C) Reserve, Reduce, Reuse

    (D) Reserve, Renewable, Recycle

20. Fossil fuels are considered non-renewable resources because they:

    (A) Can be easily reused or replaced

    (B) Cannot be easily reused or replaced

    (C) Can be broken down or decompose easily

    (D) Can take a long time to form and cannot be replaced easily

21. Which of these objects is not biodegradable?

Apple

Paper

Plastic Bottles

Leaves

22. Which of the following is a type of natural resource?
    (A) Glass
    (B) Water
    (C) Electricity
    (D) Plastic

23. Which one of these elements can be found in the crust of the earth?
    (A) Magma
    (B) Oil
    (C) Nickel
    (D) Iron

24. If the amount of smoke in the atmosphere were to reduce, which of the following would reduce also?
    (A) Oil spills
    (B) Energy
    (C) Energy costs
    (D) Air pollution

25. **'Brianne measured the temperature, rain, and wind, in the atmosphere at a certain time and place to determine its state.'**

Which of the conditions below would be described using the data?

(A) Precipitation

(B) Condensation

(C) Weather

(D) Climate

26. **'Scientists have observed that most days in The Bahamas are warm.'**

This information helps scientists find out about what concerning the country?

(A) Precipitation

(B) Condensation

(C) Weather

(D) Climate

27. What is the instrument in the picture called?

(A) A rain gauge

(B) A barometer

(C) An anemometer

(D) A hydrometer

28. What is the name given to a scientist who predicts the weather?

(A) Meteorologist

(B) Paleontologist

(C) Biologist

(D) Chemist

29. Which body revolves around planet earth?

(A) Comet

(B) Moon

(C) Stars

(D) Asteroids

30. What is the result when the earth spins on its axis?

   (A) Eclipses of the moon

   (B) Day and night

   (C) The sun's gravity

   (D) The constellation

31. The surface of which planet has the greatest percentage of oxygen?

   (A) Earth

   (B) Mars

   (C) Pluto

   (D) Neptune

32. Which of the following is an example of a physical change?

   (A) Baked cake

   (B) Burnt coal

   (C) Melted ice

   (D) Rusting bicycle frame

33. Which of the following is **NOT** a physical property of paper?

   (A) It burns

   (B) It's flat

   (C) It's white

   (D) It's smooth

34. **'Nicholas has a golf ball'**

   Which instrument can be used to measure the mass of the golf ball?

   (A) Scale

   (B) Balance

   (C) Measuring cup

   (D) Thermometer

35. A graduate cylinder measures which of the following?
    (A) Mass
    (B) Length
    (C) Volume
    (D) Temperature

36. **'Andre increased the speed during the last leg of the bike race.'**
    Based on this description, how can you describe speed?
    (A) A push, pull or lift of an object
    (B) The distance an object moves in a given amount of time
    (C) A flow of electrical charges
    (D) The change of an object's position

37. Which type of tool would be produced by wrapping an inclined plane around a pole?
    (A) Egg beater
    (B) Nutcracker
    (C) Wheelbarrow
    (D) Screw

38. Dora uses a flat head screwdriver to open a can of paint. Which simple machine is she using?
    (A) A lever
    (B) A wheel and axle
    (C) A pulley
    (D) An incline plane

39. What source is providing energy to the building in the picture?

    (A) Batteries
    (B) Generator
    (C) Solar panels
    (D) Monitor screens

40. In The Bahamas which type of vehicle would help you to save money?
    (A) A solar powered vehicle
    (B) A vehicle that runs on gasoline
    (C) An electric vehicle
    (D) A vehicle that uses natural gas

For Answer Key Go To:

http://greatminds.teachable.com/courses/glat-workbook-answer-keys/

May 2015 - Short Answer Questions

CELLS

The diagram below shows two different types of cells.

An Animal Cell

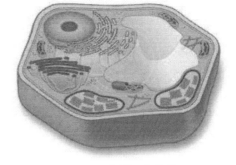

A Plant Cell

1. What is a cell?

   _____

   _____

   _____[2]

2. **'Cells must work together to perform basic life processes which helps to keep organisms alive.'**

   Name TWO life processes of cells.

   a) _____[1]

   b) _____[1]

3. **'All cells have a cell membrane.'**

   Name TWO materials that can pass through the cell membrane.

   a) _____[1]

   b) _____[1]

4. **'All cells have a nucleus.'**

   Why is the nucleus an important part of the cell?

   _____

   _____[1]

5. What is the name of the green substance found in the cells of green plants?

_____[1]

6. What would happen to the plant if the green substance found in question 5 were not present?

_____

_____

_____

_____[2]

Total Marks [10]

For Answer Key Go To:

http://greatminds.teachable.com/courses/glat-workbook-answer-keys/

PLANT GROWTH AND RESPONSE

'All living things depend on their environment to grow and be health.'

1. Name **TWO** things that must be present in order for plants to grow.

   a) _____ [1]
   b) _____ [1]

A   B

2. Write the names of the plants labeled A and B.

   (i) A _____ [1]
   (ii) B _____ [1]

3. State how each plant is able to survive in its environment.

   (i) A _____ [1]
   (ii) B _____ [1]

'The diagrams below show plants in two different environments.'

(A) Plants growing in the window   (B) Plant sitting in a cupboard

4. Explain why the plants in 'A' are growing and the plant in 'B' is dying.

_____
_____
_____
_____[2]

5. **'A plant's response to gravity is called gravitropism.'**
   Explain the term **'gravitropism'**.

_____
_____
_____
_____[2]

Total Marks [10]

For Answer Key Go To:

http://greatminds.teachable.com/courses/glat-workbook-answer-keys/

STORMS

The diagram below shows a storm.

1. **'There are many kinds of storms.'**
   How are all storms started?

   _____
   _____[1]

2. What type of storm has the strongest wind force?

   _____
   _____[1]

3. What type of weather condition would you observe if you were caught in the 'eye' of a hurricane?

   _____
   _____[1]

4. State TWO atmospheric conditions that could be experienced during a Thunderstorm.

   _____
   _____[2]

5. State TWO safety precautions that should be taken during a storm.
   (i) _____[1]
   (ii) _____[1]

6. **'Storms may have many effects in a community.'**
   Explain ONE environmental effect that a storm can have on a community.

   _____

   _____

   _____[1]

7. **'Many storms are experienced on Earth.'**
   State TWO ways in which persons are able to have fair warning before a storm occurs.

   _____

   _____

   _____[1]

Total Marks [10]

For Answer Key Go To:

http://greatminds.teachable.com/courses/glat-workbook-answer-keys/

EXPLORING SPACE

The diagrams show equipment that are used by scientists to explore and study space.

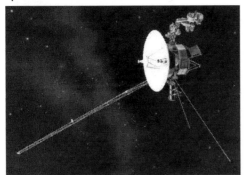

Space Probe

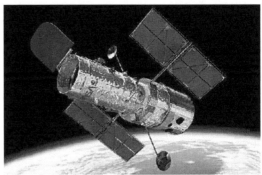

Hubble Space Telescope

Space Shuttle

Space Station

1. Read the statements then write the name of one of the objects from the objects above beneath each statement.

   a) Sends images back to earth.

   _____[1]

   b) The place where astronauts stay while in space.

   _____[1]

   c) Sends data back to earth.

   _____[1]

   d) Carries passengers and equipment to space.

   _____[1]

2. What is the name of the scientist who studies objects in space?

_____[1]

3. Give the name of one country that has done work in space.

_____[1]

4. As telescope is used to study objects in space. Name an object that a telescope helps us to see.

_____[1]

5. Explain one difference between a reflecting and a refracting telescope.

_____[1]

6. Explain how data collected from space has helped scientists on Earth.

_____

_____

_____

_____[2]

TOTAL MARKS [10]

For Answer Key Go To:

http://greatminds.teachable.com/courses/glat-workbook-answer-keys/

MIXTURES IN SOLUTIONS
The diagram shows a solution.

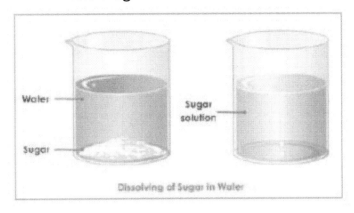

Dissolving of Sugar in Water

1. In a solution of sugar and water which substance is the:-

    Solvent _____[1]

    Solute _____[1]

2. Describe a mixture?

    _____
    _____
    _____
    _____[2]

3. (i) Other than the mixtures that are already stated in the stem of the question, give one other example of a mixture.

    _____
    _____[1]

    (ii) State TWO substances that can be found in the mixture you named in your example.

    _____
    _____[2]

4. Henry wants to use a sieve to separate a mixture of sand and pebbles.

   a) Which substance would remain in the sieve after the separation process?

   _____

   _____[2]

   b) Why was the action in 4(a) possible? Explain your answer.

   _____

   _____

   _____

   _____[2]

Total Marks [10]

For Answer Key Go To:

http://greatminds.teachable.com/courses/glat-workbook-answer-keys/

MAGNETISM

The diagram below shows various types of magnets.

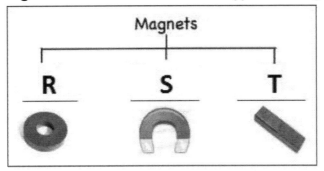

1. Name the objects labeled R, S, and T.

    R _____   [1]

    S _____   [1]

    T _____   [1]

    Observe the diagrams below.

N	S	S	N		N	S	N	S

    U   V

2. Write the letter of the diagram that is showing the magnets doing each of the following actions.

    (i) repelling_____   [1]

    (ii) attracting_____   [1]

3. How is the earth like a magnet?

    _____

    _____[1]

Use the diagram to answer question 4.

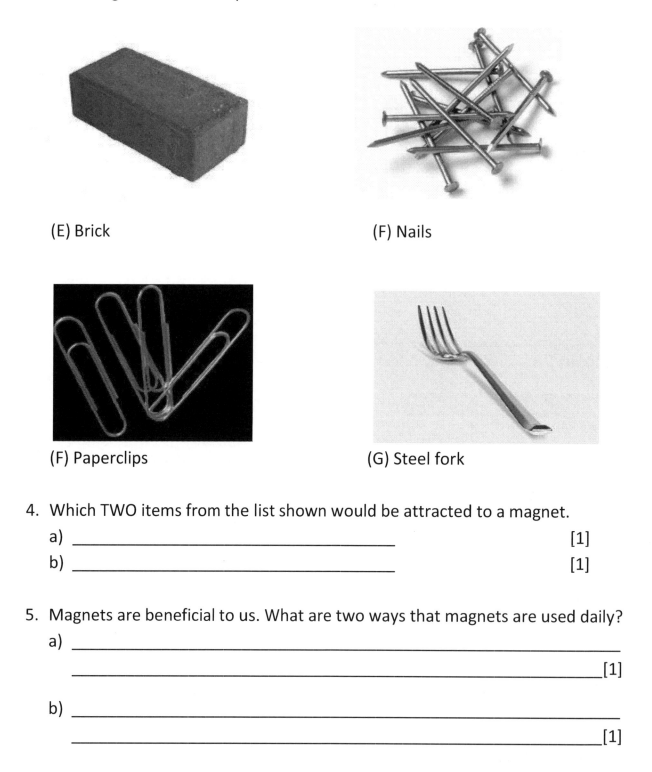

(E) Brick   (F) Nails

(F) Paperclips   (G) Steel fork

4. Which TWO items from the list shown would be attracted to a magnet.

a) _____ [1]

b) _____ [1]

5. Magnets are beneficial to us. What are two ways that magnets are used daily?

a) _____

_____[1]

b) _____

_____[1]

Total Marks [10]

May 2016 – Multiple Choice

1. The most basic unit of all living things is:
   (A) Organs
   (B) Cells
   (C) Tissues
   (D) Organ Systems

2. The 'brain' of cell is called?
   (A) Chlorophyll
   (B) Cytoplasm
   (C) Nucleus
   (D) Lysosomes

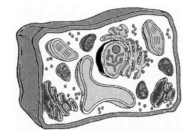

3. Choose the option that is not a characteristic of fungi.
   (A) Lives near moist areas
   (B) Decomposers
   (C) Single celled
   (D) Makes own food

4. What is the reproductive structure of fungi?
   (A) Seeds
   (B) Spores
   (C) Flowers
   (D) Pollen

5. Which option is the best definition of an invertebrate?
   (A) Animal without backbone
   (B) Animal with backbone
   (C) Animal that crawls
   (D) Animal that flies

6. Identify the group of invertebrates with poisonous threads?
   (A) Sponges
   (B) Arthropods
   (C) Reptiles
   (D) Stinging cells

7. Sponges have numerous tiny holes. What are they called?
   (A) Stomata
   (B) Pores
   (C) Vents
   (D) Spores

8. Which body system works along with the muscular system to cause movement?
   (A) Circulatory system
   (B) Respiratory system
   (C) Skeletal system
   (D) Reproductive system

9. Each bone in the body has a specific job.

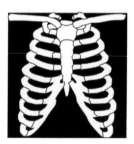

   What is the job of the bones in the picture?
   (A) To send blood to the heart and lungs
   (B) To tell the heart how to beat
   (C) To protect the heart and lungs
   (D) To send messages to the heart

10. **"Alcohol is a drug that is used by many people in The Bahamas."**

How does alcohol affect the body of a human being?

(A) Decreases movement

(B) Decreases brain activity

(C) Decreases heartbeat

(D) Decreases sleep

11. Which cells in the body fight infections?

(A) Plasma

(B) White blood cells

(C) Platelets

(D) Red blood cells

12. Which gas enters the leaf during photosynthesis?

(A) Oxygen

(B) Nitrogen

(C) Carbon monoxide

(D) Carbon dioxide

13. During the process of photosynthesis, plants create their own food. Which of the following is not required in order for photosynthesis to occur?

(A) Dirt

(B) Sunlight

(C) Chlorophyll

(D) Carbon dioxide

14. "In ecosystems, energy moves from organism to organism."

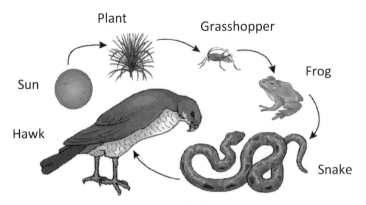

The above diagram is a representation of what?

(A) Carnivore

(B) Food chain

(C) Habitat

(D) Food web

15. **"A lion hunts and kills an antelope for food."**

What is the role of the lion in this scenario?

(A) Predator

(B) Prey

(C) Carnivore

(D) Herbivore

16. Which of the following factors affects the size of the population in an ecosystem?

(A) Average rainfall

(B) Average temperature

(C) Number and types of predators

(D) Average birthrate

17. Which of the following describes a biome?
    (A) Where they are located
    (B) The climate and types of organisms
    (C) The type of soil they consist of
    (D) How large they are

18. Where do the fewest plants grow in a Tropical Rainforest?
    (A) The canopy layer
    (B) The understory
    (C) The shrub layer
    (D) The forest floor

19. **"Very little rainfall has affected the production of plants in the dessert."**

    Which plant listed below can be found in a dessert biome?
    (A) Conifers
    (B) Cacti
    (C) Hibiscus
    (D) Dandelions

20. Which of the following is not a good way to conserve water?
    (A) Keeping the water running while brushing your teeth
    (B) Turning the shower off when it's not being used
    (C) Repairing leaking pipes
    (D) Doing full loads of laundry

21. Which two common products are made from oil?
    (A) Gasoline and diesel
    (B) Coal and natural gas
    (C) Natural gas and gasoline
    (D) Diesel and coal

22. Aerosol sprays contain what type of gases that contributes to the depletion of the ozone layer?
    (A) Chlorofluorocarbon
    (B) Hydrogen
    (C) Nitrogen
    (D) Carbon dioxide

23. What type of gas is used to cook with?
    (A) Propane
    (B) Gasoline
    (C) Methane
    (D) Fluorine

24. Which gas traps heat in the atmosphere?
    (A) Carbon dioxide
    (B) Hydrogen
    (C) Neon
    (D) Oxygen

25. Which of the following gases make up 78% of the earth's atmosphere?
    (A) Carbon dioxide
    (B) Hydrogen
    (C) Nitrogen
    (D) Oxygen

26. What does the condition of the atmosphere at a given time and place describe?
    (A) Climate
    (B) Temperature
    (C) Weather
    (D) Air Pressure

27. What is the instrument in the picture used to measure?

    (A) Wind Direction

    (B) Humidity

    (C) Rainfall

    (D) Air Pressure

28. Sarah looks at the barometer and records its reading. What is Sarah measuring?

    (A) Wind Direction

    (B) Humidity

    (C) Rainfall

    (D) Air Pressure

29. Which of the following is the largest body in the Solar System?

    (A) The Sun

    (B) The Moon

    (C) The Earth

    (D) Jupiter

30. What does the sun provide planet earth?

    (A) Light and Heat

    (B) Gas and Water

    (C) Air and Matter

    (D) Oxygen and Helium

31. If there was no sun covering the earth, what would be the result?

    (A) Only Water

    (B) Heat and Light

    (C) Living Animals and Plants

    (D) Darkness and Cold

32. The table shows a two-day weather prediction for Nassau. Based on the information in the table what is the weather condition predicted for Nassau?

TEMPERATURES IN NASSAU BAHAMAS			
	Temperature	Wind	Precipitation
Day 1	81°F	110mph	10"
Day 2	79°F	190 mph	14"

(A) Clear Skies
(B) Sunny Days
(C) Hurricane
(D) Drought

33. What is heat?
(A) Gas
(B) Energy
(C) Electricity
(D) Pollution

34. The changing of an object's position is called:
(A) Time
(B) Speed
(C) Motion
(D) Force

35. **'A metal spoon is left in a pot of boiling soup. Mother burned her finger by touching it.'**
Why did the metal spoon burn mother's finger?
(A) The spoon chemically reacted with mother's hand
(B) The spoon conducted electricity to mother's hand
(C) The spoon conducted heat to mother's hand
(D) The spoon insulated mother's hand

36. Which of the following can start or stop the movement of an object?
    (A) Mass
    (B) Motion
    (C) Force
    (D) Speed

37. Old cars can be found in a junk yard. Which of the following machines can be used to lift a car from one place to another?
    (A) A lever
    (B) A pulley
    (C) A wedge
    (D) A screw

38. A truck driver wishes to move a container onto a truck. Which simple machine should he use?
    (A) A wedge
    (B) An inclined plane
    (C) A pulley
    (D) A lever

39. Nicole wants to conserve energy in getting to school. Which of the following is the most energy efficient way of getting to school?
    (A) By bus
    (B) By car
    (C) By bicycle
    (D) By motorbike

40. Which of the following appliances uses the least amount of energy?
    (A) Can opener
    (B) Fan
    (C) Microwave
    (D) Television

May 2016 - Short Answer Questions

CELLS

The diagram below shows two different types of cells.

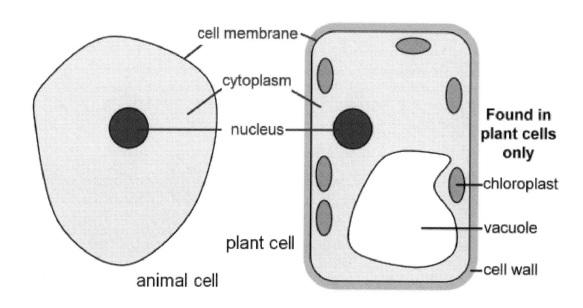

1. Other than the vacuole, name **TWO** structures found in both plant and animal cells.

   a) _____[1]

   b) _____[1]

2. State the function of the following structures of a cell.

   a) Vacuole _____[1]

   b) Cell wall_____[1]

3. Name the part of the cell that is responsible for:

   a) Controlling the activities of the cell_____[1]

   b) Allowing substances to pass in and out of the cell_____[1]

4. **'Students observed a skin cell from both an onion and a human being under the microscope.'**

   How would you be able to tell the difference between the cell that came from an onion and the one that came from the human being?

   _____

   _____[2]

5. Explain how the presence of chloroplast affects the function of a cell.

   _____

   _____

   _____[2]

                                                    Total Marks [10]

                       For Answer Key Go To:

   http://greatminds.teachable.com/courses/glat-workbook-answer-keys/

FROM FLOWER TO FRUIT

'The diagram below shows parts of a flower.'

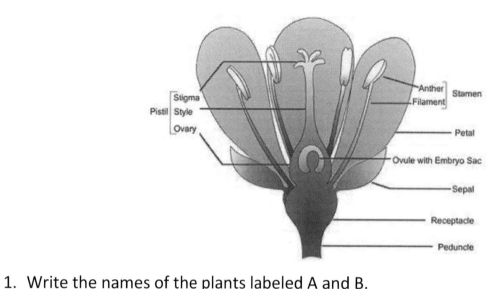

1. Write the names of the plants labeled A and B.
   (i) Makes the seeds_____[1]
   (ii) Protects the flower while in a bud_____[1]
   (iii) Provides pollen_____[1]

2. What does the ovary of a flower contain?

   _____

   _____[1]

3. What is the scientific name of a flowering plant?

   _____

   _____[1]

4. Explain one way in which pollen may be transferred from the male part of one flower to the female part of another flower.

   _____

   _____[1]

5. Name the process which occurs when pollen falls onto the pistil.

_____

_____[1]

6. Explain the importance of bees to a fruit farmer.

_____

_____[1]

7. State **TWO** ways petals help a flowering plant.

_____

_____

_____[2]

Total Marks [10]

For Answer Key Go To:

http://greatminds.teachable.com/courses/glat-workbook-answer-keys/

THE CIRCULATORY SYSTEM

The diagram below shows the circulatory system.

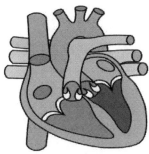

1. What is the main function of the circulatory system?

   _____
   _____[1]

2. What is the total number of chambers found in the human heart?

   _____
   _____[1]

3. Explain TWO ways the blood on the left side of the heart differs from the blood
   on the right side of the heart.
   (i) _____[1]
   (ii) _____[1]

4. Name the blood vessel responsible for the following functions.
   (i) Bringing blood to the heart _____[1]
   (ii) Taking blood away from the heart_____[1]

5. Name **TWO** things the circulation of the blood provides to the body.
   (i) _____[1]
   (ii) _____[1]

6. Explain **TWO** ways to care for the circulatory system.
   (i) _____[1]
   (ii) _____[1]

Total Marks [10]

THE ATMOSPHERE
The diagram shows the layers of the atmosphere.

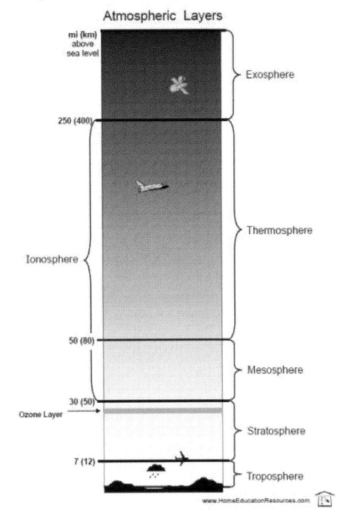

1. State the function of the atmosphere.
_____[1]

2. Name the layers of the atmosphere.
   (i)   Which contains ions_____[1]
   (ii)   Where most weather occur_____[1]
   (iii)   Where jets fly to avoid storms_____[1]

3. Name two objects found in the exosphere.

(i) _____ [1]

(ii) _____ [1]

4. 'There are many gases found in the atmosphere.'

Fill in the chart to show the gas that is found in each layer of the atmosphere.

NAME OF LAYER	USE	TYPE OF GAS
1. Troposphere	Needed by living things to survive	
2. Stratosphere	Absorbs ultraviolet rays	
3. Troposphere	Used by plants to make food	

[3]

5. State why meteors rarely reach the troposphere.

_____

_____ [2]

TOTAL MARKS [10]

For Answer Key Go To:

http://greatminds.teachable.com/courses/glat-workbook-answer-keys/

CONSERVATION OF ENERGY

The picture below encourages us to conserve energy.

1. Most energy is produced using fossil fuels.

   (i) Name a new source of energy that can be used in The Bahamas today.

   _____[1]

   (ii) Explain how this new source of energy can be used.

   _____[1]

2. Why is it important to conserve energy?

   _____[1]

3. State **TWO** uses of energy in your home.

   _____

   _____[2]

4. State **TWO** things that can be done to lower energy usage in the home.

   _____

   _____[2]

5. **'Energy cannot be created or destroyed. It can only be changed from one form to another.'**

Complete the chart to show how different devices change energy from one form to another.

DEVICE	STARTING ENERGY	ENERGY CHANGE
1. Radio	Electrical	
2. Flashlight	Chemical	
3. Toaster	Electrical	

Total Marks [10]

For Answer Key Go To:

http://greatminds.teachable.com/courses/glat-workbook-answer-keys/

SIMPLE CIRCUIT

The diagram below shows various types of magnets.

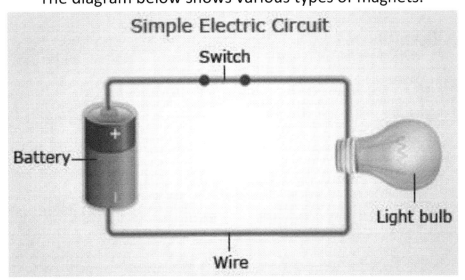

1. Name the part of the network which allows for the continuous flow of current.

   _____

   _____[1]

2. Which part of the network is responsible for supplying the energy in a simple circuit?

   _____

   _____[1]

3. In the picture above, would the light bulb be lit? Explain.

   _____

   _____[2]

4. Give one example of each of the following:
   (i) Conductor_____[1]
   (ii) Insulator_____[1]

5. Use the letters 1-4 to show the order for the flow of electricity through a circuit.

_____ Electricity travels from the power source to the bulb

_____ A switch is turned on

_____ Electricity returns to the power source

_____ The bulb lights   [2]

6. Explain what may happen to a bulb in a simple circuit if two AA batteries are replaced with three AAA batteries.

_____

_____[2]

For Answer Key Go To:

http://greatminds.teachable.com/courses/glat-workbook-answer-keys/

1. The _____ is the basic structural unit of all living things.
   (A) blood
   (B) cells
   (C) nucleus
   (D) vacuoles

2. Which of the following **NOT** present in the animal cell?
   (A) nucleus
   (B) cell wall
   (C) cell membrane
   (D) cytoplasm

3. Which of the following organisms belong to the fungi kingdom?
   (A) Bird
   (B) Mushroom
   (C) Fern
   (D) Caterpillar

4. Which atmospheric condition enhances the growth of mold onto bread?
   (A) Moist and warm conditions
   (B) Moist and cool conditions
   (C) Dry and cool conditions
   (D) Dry and warm conditions

5. Which of the following worms has unique adaptations to regrow body parts?
   (A) Planarian worms
   (B) Leech worms
   (C) Hookworms
   (D) Tape worms

6. Marlene saw a worm that had a round tube-like body with segments, a nervous system and two body openings. What kind of work did Marlene see?
   (A) Tape worm
   (B) Earth worm
   (C) Fluke worm
   (D) Hook worm

7. The circulatory system's main organ is the
   (A) Brain
   (B) Lungs
   (C) Stomach
   (D) Heart

8. The most successful habit that helps to take care of your circulatory system is
   (A) not visiting a doctor regularly
   (B) not exercising
   (C) eating a balanced diet
   (D) smoking every day

9. _____ are specialized structures that attach skeletal muscles to the bones.
   (A) Tendons
   (B) Ligaments
   (C) Blood Vessels
   (D) Muscles

10. Muscles in the heart are called
    (A) striated muscles
    (B) smooth muscles
    (C) cardiac muscles
    (D) skeletal muscles

11. 'Phototropism' is best described as which of the following statements
    (A) A plant's response to light
    (B) A plant's response to water
    (C) A plant's response to other plants
    (D) A plants response to gravity

12. Excerpt **"Different plants have different growth patterns."**
    Which statement gives the best description of the word "vine"?
    (A) a plant with a climbing stern
    (B) a plant that only grows in water
    (C) a plant with one main woody stem or trunk
    (D) a middle size plant with many stems or trunks

13. An ecosystem includes the following food chain of

If all the rabbits in the food chain die of disease, the resulting action would follow
    (A) The producer would stop producing food
    (B) The population of snakes would increase
    (C) The population of snakes would decrease
    (D) The snake would start to eat pine cones

14. Most ecosystems' main source of energy is derived from
    (A) nutrients in soil
    (B) oxygen in soil
    (C) the decomposers
    (D) light from the sun

15._____ leads to pollination when it is transferred from one flower to the next.
(A) seed
(B) fruit
(C) pollen
(D) cone

16. The flower's protective structure responsible for the male and female reproductive parts is
(A) the pistil
(B) the petal
(C) the sepal
(D) the stamen

17._____ is the amount of water vapor found in the earth's air.
(A) precipitation
(B) temperature
(C) air pressure
(D) humidity

18. Jonathon measures the amount of moisture that falls from the sky as rain, sleet, snow and hail. What process is this called?
(A) humidity
(B) air pressure
(C) precipitation
(D) temperature

19. Homes and cities are built on the earth's layer known as
(A) the inner core.
(B) the outer core.
(C) the mantle.
(D) the crust.

20. Which factors would you find in the earth's inner core?
    (A) solid, very hot metal
    (B) swirling gases
    (C) melted rock
    (D) molten, metal rock

21. The most popular star located in the center of the Solar System is the
    (A) Big Dipper.
    (B) Sun.
    (C) Orion.
    (D) North Star.

22. The planet that receives the most energy from the sun is
    (A) Uranus
    (B) Neptune
    (C) Jupiter
    (D) Mars

23. _____ is the spacecraft that sends information back to Earth
    for processing.
    (A) Space Shuttle
    (B) Space Station
    (C) Hubble Space Telescope
    (D) Space Probe

24. _____ is the instrument used to study objects in space.
    (A) Telescope
    (B) Microscope
    (C) Balance scales
    (D) Hard lens

25._____is defined as an unusual weather disturbance.
   (A) Storm
   (B) Commotion
   (C) Funnel
   (D) Condition

26.Should you be exposed to hurricane conditions outside:
   (A) lie flat on the ground
   (B) stand next to a metal light pole
   (C) run under a big tree
   (D) sit in front of your house

27.Small, solid particles of material from rocks or organisms that are moved by water or wind is the process of
   (A) erosion
   (B) sublimation
   (C) deposition
   (D) precipitation

28.Kennedy wants to compare a tennis ball's mass to a golf ball. Which of the following instruments would she use?
   (A) ruler
   (B) balance scale
   (C) microscope
   (D) telescope

29.To find the volume of baking soda, Mary would use the instrument called
   (A) a granulated cylinder
   (B) a ruler
   (C) a balance scale
   (D) a thermometer

30. Excerpt **"A Tropical conch salad is made up of a combination of conch salad and several different vegetables and fruits."** Which of the following describes a tropical conch salad:
(A) solution
(B) molecule
(C) element
(D) mixture

31. Ashley mixes lime, sugar and water together to make 'Switcha'. The sugar in the solution is referred to as
(A) ingredient
(B) solute
(C) solvent
(D) crystals

32. When a still ball begins rolling down a hill, potential energy has been changed to:
(A) electric energy
(B) kinetic energy
(C) sound energy
(D) chemical energy

33. A solar powered calculator, space probe and solar panel derives energy from:
(A) sound energy
(B) light energy
(C) electrical energy
(D) mechanical energy

34. For an electrical charge to flow _____ is needed.
(A) bulb
(B) battery
(C) circuit
(D) wire

35._____ is an example of a conductor:

(A) rubber

(B) plastic

(C) wire

(D) wood

36. Donnette turned one magnet's North Pole toward the South pole of the other. What do you think happened?

(A) They did not move.

(B) They repelled.

(C) They attracted.

(D) They pushed away.

37. Which object would a magnet attract?

(A) a crayon

(B) a ball

(C) a cinderblock

(D) a paperclip

38. A great way to conserve energy in the home is to

(A) wash a small load of clothes everyday

(B) unplug appliances not being used

(C) keep lights on

(D) leave bathroom faucets running

39. **'Conservation of energy'** is described as:

(A) The destruction and careful use of energy

(B) The unwise and careless use of energy

(C) The wise and careful use of energy

(D) The careless and wise use of energy.

40. What is the universal solvent?

    (A) Kool-Aid

    (B) Acid

    (C) Water

    (D) All liquids

For Answer Key Go To:

http://greatminds.teachable.com/courses/glat-workbook-answer-keys/

May 2017 - Short Answer Questions

MOLLUSKS

The diagram bellows shows various mollusks.

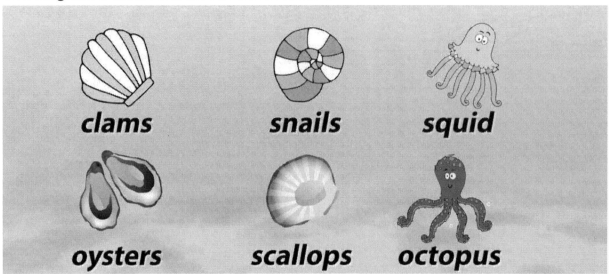

(a) Of the examples above, name a mollusk for each of the following factors:
(i) one shell
_____[1]
(ii) two shell
_____[1]
(iii) no shell
_____[1]

(b)In **TWO** ways tell how do snails and octopuses differ?
(i)_____
_____
(ii)_____
_____
[1]

(c) Give the function of the mantle mollusk.

_____

_____

[1]

(d) Give **TWO** parts of the mollusk's body other than its head.

(i)_____[1]

(ii)_____[1]

(e) **The conch is heavily incorporated into the Bahamian diet.** Give **TWO** ways we can safe guard the conch to ensure its future presence for generations to come.

_____

_____

_____

_____

_____

_____

[2]

BIOMES

Below is a picture of a Tropical Rainforest.

Identify **TWO** animals in the picture above.

(i)_____[1]

(ii)_____[1]

Give the name of the BIOME that:

(i) Receives minimal rainfall

_____[1]

(ii) Has a warm and wet climate

_____[1]

(iii) has plants with broad leaves

_____[1]

(c) (i) Which biome has a tropical climate and weather conditions like The Bahamas?

_____

_____

[1]

(c) (ii) Explain your reasons for (c)(i).

_____

_____

_____

_____

_____

_____[2]

(d) Explain how these organisms thrive in their specific biome.

(i)Sankes

_____

_____

_____[1]

(ii) Cacti

_____

_____

_____[1]

PREDICTING THE WEATHER

The picture below shows weather conditions of the atmosphere.

(a) Give **TWO** weather conditions that is occurring in the picture.

(i)_____[1]

(ii)_____[1]

(b) Give **TWO** weather instruments you will use to record the weather conditions that are shown in the diagram.

(i)_____[1]

(ii)_____[1]

(c)Who is a meteorologist?

_____

_____

[1]

(d) Weather takes place in which layer of the atmosphere?

_____

[1]

(e) Explain the difference between climate and weather.

_____

_____

_____

_____

_____

_____[2]

(f) Why is it important to know the weather conditions for each day? State **TWO** reasons.

_____

_____

_____

_____

_____

_____

_____[2]

POLLUTION

(a) What is pollution?

_____

_____

_____[1]

(b) Air can become polluted. Give **TWO** other natural resources that becomes polluted.

(i)_____[1]

(ii)_____[1]

(c) A harmful result of pollution is termed "The Greenhouse Effect".
   What causes the 'greenhouse effect'?

_____

_____[1]

Clearly express the effect that each of the following items can have on the atmosphere.

(i) Fire Extinguisher

_____
_____[1]

(ii)Refrigerator

_____
_____[1]

(iii)Air Conditioner

_____
_____[1]

(e)**Improper disposal and dumping of garbage is harmfully problematic to the environment.**

(i) How does garbage dumping affect human beings?

_____
_____
_____[1]

(ii) How does garage dumping affect animals?

_____
_____
_____[1]

(f) Offer **ONE** solution to the issue of improper dumping

_____
_____
_____[1]

(g)Explain why being environmentally friendly is important to humans.

_____

_____

_____

_____[1]

TOTAL MARKS   [10]

PHYSICAL & CHEMICAL CHANGES

(a) Give the definition for "**matte**r".

_____

_____

_____[1]

(b)Tell whether a physical or chemical change is occurring in each picture.

BAKING BREAD   PAINTING A HOUSE   MOLDED BREAD

(i) Baking Bread_____[1]

(ii)Molded Bread _____[1]

(ii) Painting a house _____[1]

(c) Billy chopped some wood. What kind of change is occurring?

_____

_____[1]

(d) Once paper is burnt, what is the new form of matter that results?

_____

_____[1]

(e) Give **TWO** physical factors of a tree and a brick of gold.

(i)_____

_____

(ii)_____

_____

[2]

(f) Zora's bicycle has not been used in years. It's been lying in her shed for 2 years. What changes have occurred:

(i)Physically

_____

_____

[1]

(ii) Chemically

_____

_____

[1]

TOTAL MARKS [10]

SIMPLE MACHINES

The picture shows a compound machine which is made up of several different simple machines.

(a) Give the name of a simple machine found on both compound machines in the photo.

_____

[1]

(b) Give the name of the simple machine being described below.

    (i) a large disc and a cylinder rod

_____[1]

    (ii) a wheel with a groove for a rope

_____[1]

(c) Simple machines are used daily.

  Describe how each simple machine is used daily.

    (i) inclined plane

_____[1]

    (ii) wheel and axle

_____[1]

(d) Sandra wants to lift a Grand Piano to the 12th floor of her condominium. The piano weighs 723 pounds. Name the simple machine that can

(i) Lift the piano through her 15 x 7 ft. day view window.

_____[1]

(ii) Bolt the piano down to the floor

_____[1]

(e)(i) Give the difference between a simple and compound machine.

_____

_____

_____

_____

[2]

(e)(ii) List an example of a compound machine.

_____

[1]

1. Which is the most basic unit of all living things?
    (A) cells
    (B) organs
    (C) systems
    (D) tissues

2. What is the importance of the nucleus of the cell?
    (A) it controls what enters and leaves the cell.
    (B) it controls the activities of the cell.
    (C) it stores food and water.
    (D) it contains a jelly like substance.

3. Some of the same structures are shared by plant and animal cells. Which structure below can only be found in plant cells?
    (A) cell wall
    (B) cytoplasm
    (C) nucleus
    (D) vacuole

4. Which part of the body is used for catching food by the animal shown in the diagram?

    (A) mantles
    (B) shells
    (C) tentacles
    (D) Tube feet

5. Which group of invertebrates are filter feeds?
   (A) echinoderms
   (B) arthropods
   (C) sponges
   (D) worms

6. Which type of muscles can only be found in the heart?
   (A) cardiac
   (B) skeletal
   (C) smooth
   (D) striated

7. Which of the following is **NOT** the proper way to care for the muscular system?
   (A) eat food containing protein
   (B) exercise regularly
   (C) eat fatty food
   (D) eat food containing calcium

8. White blood cells are the main defenders of the body. What chemicals are produced by some white blood cells?
   (A) antibodies
   (B) medicines
   (C) pus
   (D) virus

9. Daisy was attacked and stung by wasps on a nature walk. Which body system will work to allow Daisy to get well?
   (A) The Digestive System
   (B) The Immune System
   (C) The Muscular System
   (D) The Skeletal System

10. During pollination, pollen is transferred from a stamen to a _____ .
   (A) petal
   (B) pistil
   (C) ovary
   (D) sepal

11. Which part of the plant develops into a fruit?
   (A) flower
   (B) leaf
   (C) root
   (D) stem

12. What causes the plant roots to grow downward?
   (A) gravity
   (B) nutrients
   (C) soil
   (D) weeds

13. Which indigenous plant is also the national tree of The Bahamas?
   (A) Gale of Wind
   (B) Lignum Vitae
   (C) Pigeon Plum
   (D) Rooster Comb

14. Which of the following is another name by which bush medicine is known in The Bahamas?
   (A) endangered plants
   (B) flowering plants
   (C) medicinal plants
   (D) popular plants

15. You would most likely find a camel in which biome?
   (A) Deciduous forest
   (B) Desert
   (C) Taiga
   (D) Tropical Rain Forest

16. Which biome has strong sunlight, heavy rainfall and many plants and animals?
    (A) Deciduous forest
    (B) Desert
    (C) Grassland
    (D) Tropical Rain Forest

17. What is the definition of renewable?
    (A) products that can be broken down easily
    (B) products that cannot be broken down easily
    (C) resources that cannot be replaced easily
    (D) resources that can be easily replaced or reused

18. Which of the following is an example of a non-renewable resource?
    (A) air
    (B) trees
    (C) fossil fuel
    (D) water

19. Which of the following is a trace fossil?
    (A) bone
    (B) imprint
    (C) stick
    (D) track

20. What can scientists learn from fossils?
    (A) how volcanoes work
    (B) when earthquakes will happen
    (C) living things need sunlight
    (D) which organisms lived long ago

21. Which two gases make up the most of the earth's atmosphere?
    (A) hydrogen and oxygen
    (B) hydrogen and nitrogen
    (C) oxygen and carbon dioxide
    (D) oxygen and nitrogen

22. In which layer of the atmosphere would planes fly to avoid bad weather?
(A) exosphere
(B) mesosphere
(C) stratosphere
(D) troposphere

23. Which planet's surface area is shown in the picture?

(A) Earth
(B) Mars
(C) Mercury
(D) Venus

24. **'Jupiter's well-known feature is the Great Red Spot.'** What is the Great Red Spot?
(A) canyon
(B) rolling plain
(C) swirling storm
(D) volcano

25. Which of the following is an example of a fossil fuel?
(A) nuclear energy
(B) oil
(C) sunlight
(D) wind energy

26. Which fossil fuel when burned is best for the environment?
    (A) coal
    (B) natural gas
    (C) petroleum
    (D) oil

27. What is an effect of burning fossil fuel?
    (A) conservation
    (B) pollution
    (C) recycling
    (D) restoration

28. Which of the following actions would contribute to air pollution?
    (A) dumping garbage in the yard
    (B) exhaust fumes from cars
    (C) factory waste going in the sea
    (D) throwing bottles and cans into the water

29. Which body heats our surface, oceans and atmosphere?
    (A) comet
    (B) meteor
    (C) moon
    (D) sun

30. Which of the following is caused by the uneven heating of the earth's surface?
    (A) cold and warm spots
    (B) earthquakes
    (C) hot and cold spots
    (D) sunspots

31. Which of the following is an example of a wheel and axle?
    (A) axe
    (B) broom
    (C) ramp
    (D) doorknob

32. A flagpole is an example of which type of simple machine?
    (A) lever
    (B) pulley
    (C) wedge
    (D) wheel and axle

33. Which appliance shown in the diagram is a main source of light energy?

A. ☐   Blender

B. ☐   Clock

C. ☐   fan

D. ☐   torch

34. What form of energy does a ball rolling down a hill demonstrates?
    (A) kinetic energy
    (B) heat energy
    (C) light energy
    (D) potential energy

35. Which part of a simple circuit is responsible for providing the energy?
    (A) battery
    (B) lamp
    (C) switch
    (D) wire

36. **'When the switch is turned on, the path of a circuit is complete.'** What does this statement mean?
    (A) The bulb comes on because there is an open circuit.
    (B) The bulb turns off because there is an open circuit.
    (C) The bulb comes on because there is a closed circuit.
    (D) The bulb turns off because there is a closed circuit.

37. Which is an example of a physical change?
    (A) broken glass
    (B) metal rusting
    (C) paper burning
    (D) bread toasting

38. Which type of change occurs when a new substance is formed?
    (A) boiling water
    (B) chemical change
    (C) freezing water
    (D) physical change

39. Which additional source of energy uses the sun?
    (A) hydro-electric energy
    (B) wave energy
    (C) wind energy
    (D) solar energy

40. Which action shows energy conservation?
    (A) car pooling
    (B) listening to music
    (C) turning off lights
    (D) using a dishwasher

WORMS

The diagram shows three different types of worms.

Flat Worm	Round Worm	Segmented Worm

(a) Write the name of each type of worm from the box below in the correct column on the chart to complete it.

Leech	Planarian	Hookworm

[3]

(b) **'All worms are invertebrates.'**
State the main physical trait that is common to this group of animals.

_____

[1]

(c) **'A Hookworm is a parasite.'**

Give **ONE** fact to support this statement.

_____

_____

[1]

(d) 'Leaches were used by doctors in the past for medical purposes.'

Explain why the practice of using leeches for medical purposes was beneficial to human beings.

_____

_____

[1]

(e) 'Planarian worms are an exceptional group of worms.'

(i) What special trait is the planarian worm known for?

_____

_____

[1]

(ii) State the main effect that this trait has on the planarian worm population.

_____

_____

[1]

(f) 'Poor hygiene practices can cause human beings to become infected with worms.'

Explain **TWO** actions that human beings can take to avoid becoming infected with worms.

_____

_____

_____

[2]

TOTAL MARKS [10]

PLANTS

The diagram shows the food making process in green plants.

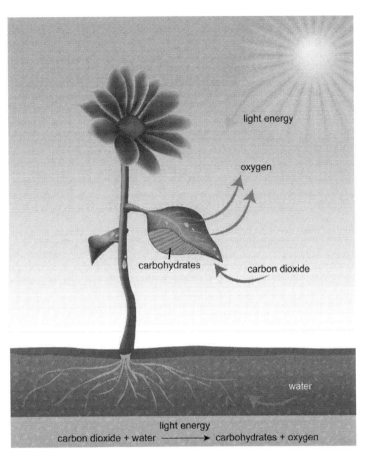

(a) What is the process of plants making their own food called?

_____

[1]

(b) List two things that are necessary for green plants to be able to make their own food.

(i) _____ [1]

(ii) _____ [1]

(c) (i) What waste product is created as a direct result of green plant making its own food?

_____ [1]

(c) (ii) Explain **ONE** way in which the waste product produced in the plant food-making process is important to human beings?

_____ [1]

(d) Explain how glucose (sugar) is made.

_____

_____

_____

_____

[2]

(e) State the function of the leaves and roots in plants.

(i)   Leaves _____ [1]

(ii)   Roots _____ [1]

(f) What is the name of the tiny holes which are mostly found on the under surface of plant leaves.

_____ [1]

TOTAL MARKS [10]

The diagram shows a system of the human body.

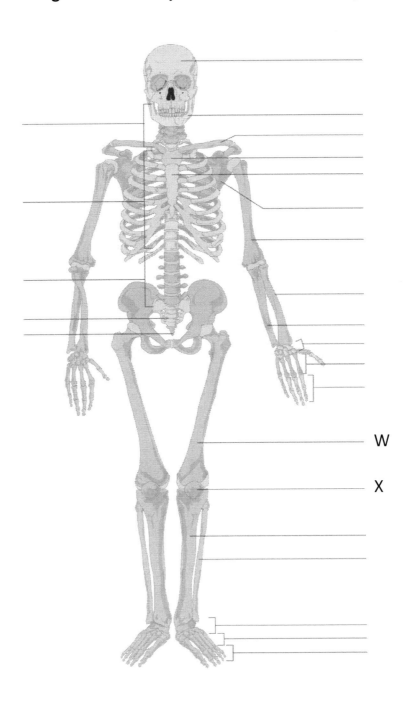

W

X

(a) Give the scientific name of the system shown.

_____

_____

[1]

(b) Name the bone structures of the diagram that are labelled 'W' and 'X'.

W _____

X _____   [2]

(c) State **TWO** functions of the human body system shown above.

(i) _____

_____

(ii) _____

_____

[2]

(d) **'Joints allows the human body to make different kinds of movement.'**

Which joint in the human body is responsible for helping the body to carry out back and forth movements?

_____

[1]

(e) 'Bones meet at joints where they are attached to each other.'

Define the term **'joints'**.

_____

_____

_____

[2]

(f) What is one way in which the rib cage helps the human body?

_____

_____

[1]

(g) How many bones does the adult human skeleton have?

_____

_____

[1]

TOTAL MARKS [10]

HURRICANES

The diagram shows the varying sections of a hurricane.

'In 2019 The Bahamas experienced a major hurricane named Dorian.'

(a) What is a hurricane?

_____ [1]

(b) In which type of water can hurricanes be formed?

_____ [1]

'Weeks before a hurricane is scheduled to affect The Bahamas, weather forecasters warn the residents about it.'

(c) What is the scientific name of the scientist who provides information about changing weather conditions in a country?

_____ [1]

(d) **'All hurricanes are given names.'** Explain why is this process necessary?

_____

_____

_____

[2]

(e) What is the name of **ONE** extreme weather condition that can be experienced during a hurricane?

_____

[1]

(f) What are **TWO** ways in which people can prepare for a hurricane?

(i) _____

(ii) _____

[2]

(g) Explain **TWO** negative effects that hurricanes can have on our islands.

(i) _____

_____

(ii) _____

_____

[2]

TOTAL MARKS [10]

MOTION AND FORCES

The picture below shows force and motion.

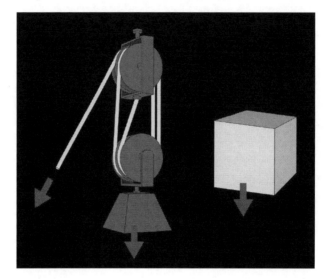

(a) Define the term **'motion'**.

_____

_____

[2]

(b) **'Most forces will cause an object to move.'**

Name **TWO** ways in which you can apply force to an object.

1. _____

2. _____

[2]

(c) **'One way to describe the motion of an object is its speed.'**

What is speed?

_____ [2]

(d) State which type of force contributes to each of the following actions:

(i) slows down an object when it comes into contact with another object

_____ [1]

(ii)   pulls objects towards each other and hold you on Earth

_____ [1]

Use the picture to answer questions (e) (i) & (e) (ii).

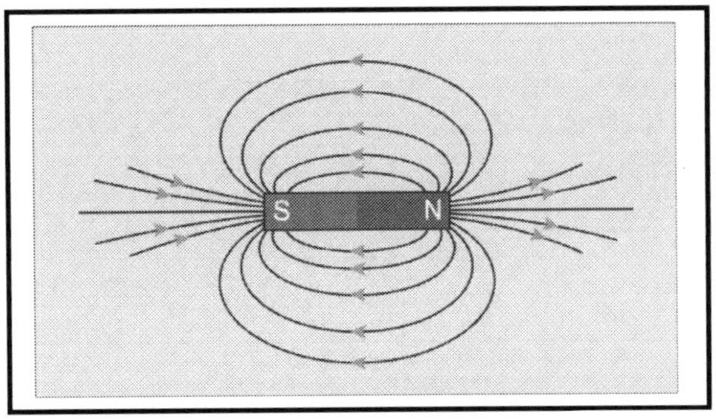

'The diagram shows a bar magnet.'

(e) (i) What are the lines around the bar magnet called?

_____ [1]

(e) (ii) What do we call the ends of the magnet?

_____ [1]

TOTAL MARKS [10]

MATTER

The diagram shows instruments that are used to measure matter.

(a) 'Matter is anything that has mass and takes up space.'

(i) Define the term **'mass'**.

_____

_____

[1]

(ii) Name the instrument that is used to measure **'mass.'**

_____

_____

[1]

(iii)   Name **TWO** other quantities that we can measure.

_____

_____

[2]

(b) 'Tanya placed some water in a graduated cylinder. The water measured 100 C.C. She then dropped a rock into the cylinder which sank to the bottom of the water.'

What happens to the level of the water when the rock is placed inside the graduated cylinder?

_____

_____

[1]

(c) What would be the best instrument to measure each of the following items?

(i) the length of your notebook _____ [1]

(ii) a cup of water _____ [1]

(iii) the mass of a tennis ball _____ [1]

(d) (i) What is temperature?

_____

_____

[1]

(d) (ii) State the name of the instrument that is used to measure temperature?

_____

[1]

TOTAL MARKS [10]

May 2019 – Multiple Choice

1. What is the basic unit of life called?

    A. ☐ Cells
    B. ☐ Germination
    C. ☐ Matter
    D. ☐ Pollination

2. Which two structures shown below can only be found in the plant cell?

    A. ☐ Chloroplast and vacuole
    B. ☐ Chloroplast and nucleus
    C. ☐ Cell wall and chloroplast
    D. ☐ Nucleus and vacuole

3. Fungi are important to an ecosystem as they are _____.

    A. ☐ consumers
    B. ☐ decomposers
    C. ☐ producers
    D. ☐ regulators

4. Which type of fungus is used to make penicillin?

    A. ☐ mildew
    B. ☐ mold
    C. ☐ Mushroom
    D. ☐ yeast

5. Which of the following is a crustacean?

    A. ☐ chicken
    B. ☐ crab
    C. ☐ shark
    D. ☐ spider

6. Which one is **NOT** a characteristic of a crustacean?

    A. ☐ Scaly skin
    B. ☐ invertebrate
    C. ☐ Can swim
    D. ☐ exoskeleton

7. Which body part is used by the animal in the diagram for feeding and movement?

    A. ☐ shell
    B. ☐ mantle
    C. ☐ Tube feet
    D. ☐ tentacles

8. Which one is a characteristic of the group echinoderm?

    A. ☐ Stinging cells
    B. ☐ Spiny skin
    C. ☐ Soft fleshy body
    D. ☐ Jointed legs

9. Which animals belongs to the echinoderm group?

    A. ☐ Jellyfish
    B. ☐ Sea star
    C. ☐ Octopus
    D. ☐ Whelk

10. What is the scientific name given to flowering plants?

    A. ☐ angiosperm
    B. ☐ germination
    C. ☐ monocots
    D. ☐ pollination

11. Which structure is the male part of the flower?

    A. ☐ petal
    B. ☐ pistil
    C. ☐ sepal
    D. ☐ stamen

12. Rain forests make _____ for the world.

    A. ☐ rubber
    B. ☐ chocolate
    C. ☐ oxygen
    D. ☐ rain

13. The climate in a deciduous forest _____.

    A. ☐ Stays the same all year.
    B. ☐ Ranges from cold in winter to warm in summer.
    C. ☐ Is always cold and dry.
    D. ☐ Is humid and warm.

14. **Each bone has a job to do.** What is the job of the spine?

    A. ☐ To pump blood through the body
    B. ☐ To tell the brain what to do
    C. ☐ To protect the spinal cord
    D. ☐ To protect the ribs

15. Which is a function of the skeletal system?

    A. ☐ To transport gases
    B. ☐ To get rid of waste
    C. ☐ To give the body support
    D. ☐ To send nerve signals

16. **A vulture eats animals that are dead and rotting**. Which term best describes the vulture?

A. ☐ scavenger
B. ☐ producer
C. ☐ predator
D. ☐ decomposer

17. In an ecosystem energy moves from one organism to another organism. Which organism is a producer?

A. ☐ hawk
B. ☐ grass
C. ☐ snake
D. ☐ frog

18. Which term best describes humidity?

A. ☐ Moving air
B. ☐ Water vapor in the air
C. ☐ How hot or cold something is
D. ☐ The pressing of air

19. **'Susie looks at her barometer and records her reading.'** What is Susie measuring?

A. ☐ Temperature
B. ☐ Precipitation
C. ☐ Humidity
D. ☐ Air pressure

20. Which instrument is used to measure precipitation?

A. ☐ Wind vane
B. ☐ barometer
C. ☐ anemometer
D. ☐ Rain gauge

21. In which layer of the atmosphere does most weather changes occur?

A. ☐ Troposphere
B. ☐ Mesosphere
C. ☐ Stratosphere
D. ☐ Thermosphere

22. Which storm can form anytime of the year?

A. ☐ hurricane
B. ☐ tornado
C. ☐ blizzard
D. ☐ thunderstorm

23. What happens when a hurricane moves over land?

A. ☐ Its eye expands.
B. ☐ It loses strength.
C. ☐ It gains strength.
D. ☐ It disappears.

24. What is the largest body in the solar system?

A. ☐ Jupiter
B. ☐ Earth
C. ☐ Mars
D. ☐ Sun

25. What are stars mainly made of?

A. ☐ water
B. ☐ rocks
C. ☐ gases
D. ☐ dust

26. Look at the space craft. What is it used for?

A. ☐ Sending images back to earth.
B. ☐ Sending data back to earth.
C. ☐ To house astronauts.
D. ☐ Carrying passengers.

27. Scientists who study stars and objects in space are called _____.

A. ☐ Paleontologists
B. ☐ Meteorologists
C. ☐ Astronomers
D. ☐ Astronauts

28. Which instrument is used to study objects in space?

A. ☐ Microscope
B. ☐ Telescope
C. ☐ Compass
D. ☐ Space station

29. Which of the following is an example of a non-renewable resource?

A. ☐ wind
B. ☐ water
C. ☐ coal
D. ☐ vegetation

30. To preserve resources for the future, what do we need to do?

A. ☐ Use them wisely
B. ☐ Use them more frequently
C. ☐ Look for more
D. ☐ Consume more of them

31. Which of the following can be measured using a thermometer?

A. ☐ Wind speed
B. ☐ temperature
C. ☐ radiation
D. ☐ Light

32. What is the boiling point of water on the Celsius scale?

A. ☐ 212 degrees Fahrenheit
B. ☐ 32 degrees Fahrenheit
C. ☐ 100 degrees Celsius
D. ☐ 0 degrees Celsius

33. Which of the following shoes potential energy?

A. ☐ Water flowing
B. ☐ A child playing football
C. ☐ A parked car
D. ☐ A burning log

34. What kind of energy is shown by a ball rolling down a hill?

A. ☐ Wind energy
B. ☐ Potential energy
C. ☐ Kinetic energy
D. ☐ Heat energy

35. What is motion?

   A. ☐ The energy to do something
   B. ☐ The ability to do work
   C. ☐ Change in position
   D. ☐ A push or pull

36. Which is an example of a force being applied to something?

   A. ☐ Watching television
   B. ☐ Standing on a hill
   C. ☐ Reading a book
   D. ☐ Pulling a wagon

37. What is the space around a magnet called?

   A. ☐ Static electricity
   B. ☐ sphere
   C. ☐ Magnetic poles
   D. ☐ Magnetic field

38. What happens when two south poles of a magnet are placed together?

   A. ☐ They weaken
   B. ☐ They repel
   C. ☐ They become stronger
   D. ☐ They attract

39. Which process results in a chemical change?

   A. ☐ tearing
   B. ☐ cutting
   C. ☐ burning
   D. ☐ boiling

40. Which change in matter is easiest to reverse?

A. ☐ Milk souring
B. ☐ Leaves burning
C. ☐ Iron rusting
D. ☐ Chocolate melting

SPONGES

The diagram shows several different types of sponges.

(a) List **TWO** traits of sponges.

_____

_____

_____

[2]

(b) (i) Explain how sponges get their food.

_____

_____

_____

[2]

(ii) What is the name that is given to sponges because of how they feed?

_____

[1]

(c) Write **'TRUE'** of **'FALSE'** to confirm each statement.

     (i)   Sponges have a skeleton   _____   [1]

     (ii)   Sponges do not have a backbone_____   [1]

(d) Give the name of one place in the waters of The Bahamas where sponges can be found.

_____

     [1]

(e) Name two ways that a natural sponge may be used around the house.

     (i)   _____

_____

     [1]

     (ii)   _____

_____

     [1]

THE CIRCULATORY SYSTEM
The diagram shows an organ that is found in the human body.

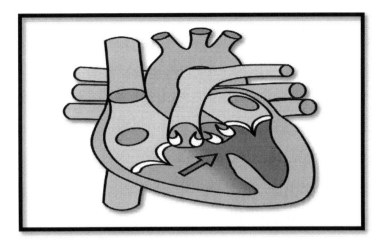

(a) (i) What is the name of the organ that is shown in the diagram above?

_____

[1]

(ii) What is the main function of the organ that you named in (a) (i)?

_____

[1]

(b) Fill in the empty boxes to complete the table below on types of blood vessels.

Function/Type of blood vessels	Name of the blood vessels
(i) Smallest blood vessels	
(ii) Carries blood to the heart	
(iii) Carries blood away from the heart	

[3]

(c) (i) What is the name of the partition that separates the right side of the heart from the left side of the heart?

_____

[1]

(ii) Explain why this partition is important in the heart.

_____

[1]

(d) Name **TWO** ways to keep your heart healthy.

(i)   _____

(ii)   _____

[2]

(e) State why it is important for you not to touch someone else's blood with your bare hands.

_____

[1]

PLANT GROWTH AND RESPONSE
The diagram shows a growing plant.

(a) Name **TWO** things plants need to grow.

(i) _____ [1]

(ii) _____ [1]

(b) **'Different plants have different growth patterns'.** Which types of plants have the following features?

(i)   climbing stems   _____ [1]

(ii)   one main woody stem   _____ [1]

(iii) are middle sized with many stems and trunks

_____ [1]

(iv) Explain what a stimuli is.

_____

_____

[1]

(v) Name **TWO** stimuli that plants respond to.

- _____ [1]
- _____ [1]

(vi) Explain why plants grow towards the light.

_____

_____

_____

_____

EARTH'S LAYERS
The diagram shows the layers of the earth.

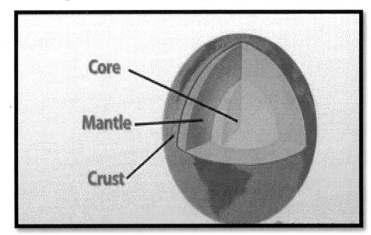

(a) Name the layer of the earth that:

    (i)   has most of the earth's mass   _____ [1]

    (ii)   we live on   _____ [1]

    (iii)   has both a liquid and a solid section_____[1]

(b) What is the name of the melted rock that flows out into the Earth's crust?

_____

[1]

(c) **"The outer core of the earth is liquid because of extreme heat but the inner core is solid'.** Explain why the inner core of the earth is solid and not liquid.

_____

_____

_____

[2]

(d) Name **TWO** parts of the earth's crust.

(i) _____ [1]

(i) _____ [1]

(e) **Scientists study the crust of the earth by drilling into the surface layer'.**

State **TWO** other ways that scientists are able to study the other layers

of the earth.

(i) _____ [1]

(ii) _____ [1]

WEATHERING AND EROSION

The diagram below shows different types of weathering.

(a) (i) Define the term **'weathering'**.

_____

[1]

(ii) State **ONE** difference between the actions of weathering and erosion.

_____

[1]

(b) **'A tree is growing on a rock which caused the rock to crack'.**
Explain why the rock cracked.

_____

_____

[2]

(c) List **TWO** agents of erosion.

(i) _____ [1]

(ii) _____ [1]

(d) State how both weathering and erosion affects Earth's surface.

_____

[1]

(e) **Earthquakes cause rapid changes on earth.** What is an earthquake?

_____

[1]

(f) What is the name of the scale that is used to measure an earthquake?

_____

[1]

(g) Explain the difference between magma and lava.

_____

_____

_____

_____

_____

[2]

MIXTURES AND SOLUTIONS

The diagram shows pictures of mixtures and solutions.

(i)

(ii)

(a) State whether each diagram shown is a **mixture** or a **solution**.

   (i) _____ [1]

   (ii) _____ [1]

(b) (i)   Define the term '**dissolve**'.

          _____ [1]

   (iii)   State **ONE** factor that affects the rate at which a substance dissolves.

          _____ [1]

(c) State **TWO** properties of mixtures.

_____

_____

_____

[2]

(d) **'Water and salt were combined to form a solution'.** From the solution, name the solute and the solvent.

   (i) solute _____ [1]

   (ii) solvent _____ [1]

(e) (i) Would a pencil be classified as a mixture or a solution?

_____

[1]

(ii) Explain your answer from (e)(i)

_____

_____

_____

[1]

REFERENCES

1. Ministry of Education, Examination and Assessment Division, Grade Level Assessment Test – 6, Science May 2011

2. Ministry of Education, Examination and Assessment Division, Grade Level Assessment Test – 6, Science May 2012

3. Ministry of Education, Examination and Assessment Division, Grade Level Assessment Test – 6, Science May 2013

4. Ministry of Education, Examination and Assessment Division, Grade Level Assessment Test – 6, Science May 2014

5. Ministry of Education, Examination and Assessment Division, Grade Level Assessment Test – 6, Science May 2015

6. Ministry of Education, Examination and Assessment Division, Grade Level Assessment Test – 6, Science May 2016

7. Ministry of Education, Examination and Assessment Division, Grade Level Assessment Test – 6, Science May 2017

8. Ministry of Education, Examination and Assessment Division, Grade Level Assessment Test – 6, Science May 2018

9. Ministry of Education, Examination and Assessment Division, Grade Level Assessment Test – 6, Science May 2019